30 Varied Rambles
in Warwickshire
and Worcestershire

30 Varied Rambles in Warwickshire and Worcestershire

The bell tower, Evesham, from the west

Drawings by Jenny Taylor

Published in England by
Thornhill Press
24 Moorend Road
Cheltenham
MCMLXXXIX

ISBN 0 946328 23 4

PLEASE RESPECT THE COUNTRY CODE

Printed by Billing & Sons Ltd, Worcester.

INTRODUCTION

Our third book of selected rambles is based on similar principles to the other two. The walks which are numbered in the table of contents and on the back cover, are all circular and include items of historical, architectural or antiquarian interest.

In answer to many requests we have included a good number of easy, short walks which can be comfortably undertaken in a morning or an afternoon, and which we think are also suited for family outings. The itineraries of Warwick, Stratford, Alcester, Evesham, Worcester and Bewdley we believe add interest and variety to the book. In every case we have endeavoured to find a place of refreshment where we have enjoyed good food and drink.

The greatest care has been taken in compiling this book of rambles. The maps and route details should be adequate, but we do recommend the use of the popular Landranger O.S. 1:50,000 sheets or the Pathfinder 1:25,000 series which indicate the rights of way and can add much interest to the rambles. The map required is stated at the beginning of each walk and the O.S. grid reference for the starting point is given.

We hope you will find the footpaths as we have described them, but we cannot be held responsible if changes have taken place. Footpaths are sometimes ploughed out and the routes diverted, signposts and waymarks can be removed, stiles can fall into decay and are not always replaced, and footpaths which are not walked regularly can become overgrown and obscured in the summer months.

Finally our thanks once more to Jenny who has provided all the drawings, to Brian who has assiduously checked the right of way on the maps, to Max, Geoff, Jim, Moira, Tom, Tony and Cis, our patient, faithful walking companions, and Mollie and Beryl who have read through the text.

CONTENTS

ILLUSTRATIONS

Preamble to the Warwickshire Walks

Warwickshire — 'mid-most England' — traditionally renowned for its small medieval towns, its quaint villages with timber-framed, thatched cottages, its winding leafy lanes, and verdant pastoral meadows, has lost most of its industrialised, densely urbanised areas, and, thanks to the local government reorganisation of 1974, is once more a rural county. Though rather flat or at best only gently undulating, and with much land given over to intensive agriculture, the Warwickshire countryside has nevertheless considerable attractions for the rambler.

The Avon valley enjoys an early Spring, an advantage exploited by many generations of market gardeners in the Vale of Evesham and a natual phenomenon which attracts a number of less common migrant song-birds, — nightingales, nightjars, marsh warblers, wood warblers, white throats, red-backed shrikes, spotted fly-catchers and cirl buntings, as well as the old familiars.

'The ousel-cock, so black of hue,
With orange-tawny bill,
The throstle with his note so true,
The wren with little quill,
The finch, the sparrow and the lark,
The plain-song cuckoo grey.'
                    (Midsummer Night's Dream. Act III Sc. i)

In recent summers kingfishers have been seen once more, garden warblers have been heard, and there have been several reports of sightings of quail.

Despite the ravages of the Dutch elm disease the county still has a fair amount of woodland, and thanks to the tireless efforts of the Warwickshire Nature Conservation Trust, is managing to preserve much of what remains. A good deal of the woodland here is the legacy of the ancient practice of coppicing oak, ash, hazel and field maple, which has created woods which are carpeted with Spring and Summer flowers. Here we can find not only bluebells, primroses, wood anemones and wood sorrel, but helleborine, purple and spotted orchids, yellow archangel, woodruff, agrimony, figwort, and sometimes even the rare herb paris. To walk in a Warwickshire wood in the early morning of a bright May day is to have that wonderful 'life is so good' feeling. The air is filled with the heady scent of a million bluebells and throbs with beautiful, passionate birdsong.

The river Avon meanders sleepily through a countryside steeped in history . Two superb medieval castles dominate Warwick and Kenilworth. A host of historic houses, open to the public, − Arbury Hall, Baddesley Clinton House, Charlecote Park, Coughton Court, Farnborough House, Packwood House, Ragley Hall, Upton House − together provide a graphic panorama of English domestic history and architecture, while the parklands of the houses are the epitome of everything that has long been admired in the English countryside.

Warwickshire is equally rich in ecclesiastical architecture. There are 254 medieval churches most of which had been built by the early 13th century, and several can provide fine examples of Norman, Decorated and Perpendicular styles of church building.

There are counties where the scenery is more dramatic or picturesque, but none which has produced a greater splendour of striking historic personalities, has so consistently determined national taste, or played such a decisive role in the course of the nation's history. At the heart of England, Warwickshire was always deeply involved in the nation's internal struggles. Kenilworth was the centre of the civil war associated with Simon de Montfort in the 13th century, it was also the scene of Edward II's humiliation and abdication in the 14th century, and of the princely pleasures of the court of Elizabeth I and her favourite Robert Dudley, Earl of Leicester, in the 16th century. At the tomb of Richard Beauchamp in his chantry chapel at Warwick, we are close to the Hundred Years War of the 15th century. On the 23rd of October, 1642 on the slopes of Edge Hill, Royalists and Parliamentarians slaughtered each other in the first real battle of the Civil War.

It is in the villages of Warwickshire that the true nature of the county is found. Some were originally clearings or hilltop settlements in the great Forest of Arden and continue to proclaim it in their names. Others were to provide homes and estates for the gentry, as at Coughton where the fortunes of the Throckmortons recall the bitter religious strife of the Elizabethan and early Stuart era. At Charlecote the Lucys were able to combine house, river and parkland in perfect harmony.

In such places it is possible to find quiet and peace, time to reflect and admire the scene away from the stress of nearby conurbations.

'And this our life exempt from public haunt,
Finds tongues in trees, books in running brooks,
Sermons in stones and good in everything,
I would not change it.'

(As You Like It. Act II Sc.i)

WALK 1
A Walk Around Warwick

Warwick, at the very heart of England, is a fascinating county town of consider local importance. Much of its visual attraction results from its development in the Middle Ages being determined by the building of a castle near the river Avon in 1068, and the subsequent erection of the town walls so that its main streets ran north and south, east and west between the town gates. Moreover a great fire in 1694 removed a clutter of largely timbered houses in the centre and made space for fine new buildings in brick and stone in the 18th century. Fortunately most of the important medieval structures — the Castle, St. John's House, the East and West gates were untouched by the fire.

Celia Fiennes who visited Warwick in 1697 clearly recognised the benefit of the calamity.

'The town of Warwick by means of a sad fire about 4 or 5 years since that laid the greater part in ashes, its most now new buildings which is with brick and coyn'd with stone and the windows the same; there still remains some few houses of the old town which are all built of stone; the streets are very handsome and the buildings regular and fine, not very lofty being limited by act of parliament to such a pitch and size to build the town.'
(Journeys of Celia Fiennes — edited Christopher Morris p.114)

Daniel Defoe coming to Warwick in 1720 was of the same opinion.

'As to the town of Warwick, it is really a fine town, pleasantly situated on the bank of the Avon, over which there is a large and stately bridge, the Avon being grown now a pretty large river, Warwick was ever esteemed a handsome well-built town, and there were several good houses in it, but the face of it is now quite altered; for having been almost wholly reduced to a heap of rubbish by a terrible fire, about two and twenty years ago, it is now rebuilt in so noble and so beautiful a manner that few towns in England make so fine an appearance.'
(A Tour Through the Whole Island of Great Britain — p.405.)

Time spent in a leisurely itinerary of the town is amply rewarded.

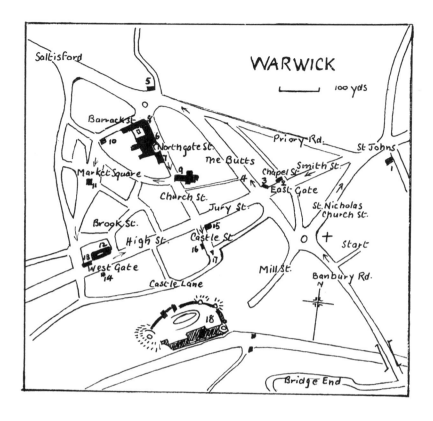

From the car park in St. Nicholas' park walk right along Banbury Road past St. Nicholas' Church which was built in 1780 by a Warwick architect Thomas Johnson. The present building replaced an early church which in turn had been built on the site of a nunnery destroyed in a Danish raid. To-day the church is no longer used for services and is only of interest as an early example of the Gothic revival in church architecture.

Continue to the right along St. Nicholas Church Street which still has some timber-framed houses, to reach St. John's House near the traffic lights at Coten End.

1. St. John's House. This handsome Jacobean stone mansion stands on the site of the hospital of St. John the Baptist founded in 1175 by

Landor House, Warwick

William de Newburgh, Earl of Warwick, to provide 'casual lodging and refreshment to poor wayfarers and more permanent help to the local poor and infirm'. After the Dissolution, in 1540 the hospital was granted to a royal servant Anthony Stoughton, whose initials 'A. S.' and the date 1626 appear inside the present house. Despite considerable alterations it remains a most elegant building with its symmetrical front, neatly shaped gables and stone mullioned windows. The splendid wrought iron gates supported by sturdy gate piers, were probably the work of Nicholas Paris, a noted Warwick smith of the early 18th century.

The house has seen many uses through the years, being in the late 18th century an Academy 'For the Education of Young Gentlemen who are genteelly Boarded, tenderly and affectionately treated, Liberally Educated, and moderately Charged. Board and Lodging, per annum, with a Bedfellow Twelve Guineas, In a single Bed Fourteen Guineas'.

In the 19th century St. John's accommodated the Conservative Association, and provided lodging for the parish clerk of St. Nicholas church. In the present century it has been the Army Pay

Office, the Infantry Records Office, and to-day serves as part of the Warwickshire Museum and Royal Warwickshire Regimental Museum. Admission is free and it is well worth a visit.

From St. John's House walk up Smith Street which in the Middle Ages was occupied by armourers, black and white smiths and other 'noisome trades' largely employed by the castle. In 1539 Leland observed that some Jews were to be found here and when in 1656 the Commonwealth Council allowed Jews to own property in England, a number of Jewish families settled in Smith Street.

2. Landor House. At the top of the street where it joins Chapel Lane is Landor House, built in 1692 by Roger Hurlbutt, in brick with strong stone quoins and of two storeys with a hipped roof. The eye-catching doorway with a segmental pediment in brackets which at first sight appears to be wood, is in fact painted stone and was probably designed by Sir William Wilson who drew up the plans for the rebuilding of St. Mary's after the fire.

Walter Savage Landor, writer of belles lettres, was born here in 1775. Since 1879 the house and the adjoining timber-framed cottages have been occupied by the King's High School for Girls.

3. The East Gate. This is one of the surviving gates of the medieval town. Above is the chapel of St. Peter built in the first half of the 15th century to replace a much older chapel. It was given its Gothic features including the delightful miniature turret-lantern in 1788 by a local architect, Francis Hiorne, one-time mayor of Warwick and a great enthusiast for Georgian Gothic. To-day the chapel is used by the King's High School.

Directly opposite Landor House is East Gate Cottage, a pleasing, neat timber-framed house with three gables and the date 1686 on the rainwater head.

Through the vaulted pedestrian arch and on the left is a Greek Doric cast-iron Victorian pillar box with a vertical aperture, an interesting survival most carefully preserved, together with its fellow at the West Gate.

Continue the itinerary along the Butts to the right and follow what was the line of the medieval town wall from the East Gate to the North Gate. Alas, the walls were largely in ruins when Leland visited the town in 1539. The name The Butts is a relic of the statute of Edward III which required archery butts to be set up in towns, where able-bodied men over the age of fifteen were required to practise with the long bow on Sundays and feast days. After about fifty yards there is a narrow entry on the left.

4. This was once called Canon Row and more recently known locally as Tink-a-tank Lane, a delightful onomatopoeic name from the days when wooden pattens or clogs worn by Warwick folk made such a sound as they pattered along the narrow paved passage between the high stone walls.

At the top of the Butts and facing Northgate Street close to where the town's North Gate once stood is

5. Northgate House. According to the date on the rainwater head this striking building was completed in 1698 and was originally two houses with a shared carriage-way running under the pediment in the centre, suggesting that it may have been intended as a coaching inn. It is brick built with stone quoins and has a painted sundial in an oval cartouche set above the central carriage-arch. At the side of the house on the Cape Road there is a fine projecting, corbelled sundial also dated 1698. Over the wall at the rear of the builing is a neat, hidden garden which was designed by Edwin Reynolds, an architect who lived here between the World Wars.

Northgate Street is the finest street in Warwick and arguably one of the most handsome Georgian streets in England. The east side is a terrace of attractive Georgian houses, now largely offices of the Warwickshire County Council; on the west side stands the Shire Hall, the Judge's Lodgings, and what until the middle of the 19th century was the County Gaol.

Designed by Sanderson Miller, an amateur architect of Radway Grange, the Shire hall was built by Warwick builders David and William Hiorne and Job Collins between 1755 and 1758,

6. Warwick Shire Hall is altogether an impressive building. A one-storey structure originally in red sandstone, now refaced in white Staffordshire stone, the outer walls are punctuated with columns and pilasters with Corinthian capitals, whilst the pediments are nicely offset with a rich carved garland frieze. The overall result is distinctly impressive without being pompous.

The interior of the Hall is delightful. It is 93 feet by 34, stone faced and carries the familiar Corinthian pilasters and garland frieze. Suspended from the coffered ceiling is a series of magnificent chandeliers. The walls are further adorned with ancient javelins which formerly were carried by the guards who accompanied the High Sheriff and the Judges of Assize to the customary Assize service at St. Mary's Church.

The two courts adjoining were designed to be open to the hall like those in the Guild Hall at Worcester. The judges and law clerks disliked this arrangement and the courts were enclosed with partitions in 1780. Each court is octagonal in design and has free-standing Corinthian columns with a gallery behind. Each is lit from a lantern topping a domed ceiling which has crisp foliage in stucco. To-day they are in regular use as Crown Courts. In the 18th century the right-hand court heard criminal cases, the left-hand one civil cases.

7. The Judge's Lodging adjoining the Shire Hall on the south side was built much later in 1815, designed by Henry Hakewill in the neo-classical style.

8. Until 1860, the County Gaol stood on the north side of the Shire Hall. It was built in 1780 by Thomas Johnson in a rather austere neo-classical style using less ornamental Tuscan Doric pilasters. Rebuilt and modernised, it is now used as offices by the County Council.

Through the archway in the courtyard on the left is a grassy mound. On the top is the ceiling aperture of the silo-like dungeon which dates from the 17th century. The dungeon is reached down 31 steps from the cell block beneath the courts. It is brick-built and circular, with a floor sloping from the sides to the cesspit in the centre. A series of wooden stakes at intervals around the cesspit carry metal staples through which the chain was passed which was attached to the prisoner's leg-irons. The chain was then drawn up the stairway and padlocked to a stout metal ring in the wall outside the door.

John Howard, visiting Warwick Gaol in 1775, found 52 prisoners chained in this dungeon, 'two of whom were ill of a slow fever'. He continued, 'From the aperture of this dungeon the steam of the prisoners' breath comes out, in winter, like the smoke of a chimney'.

In 1661 George Fox found 50 Quakers confined in this vile place for refusing to take the oath of allegiance to Charles II.

Around the corner in Barrack Street, called in the 18th century Bridewell Lane, is preserved inserted in the wall, a cell door of the original gaol. In the middle of Barrack Street the centre archway which is now blocked up was the entrance to the Bridewell. Immediately inside on the right stood the Gaoler's Lodge and above was the Death Cell where condemned prisoners awaited execution in the street outside.

There still remain inserted in the stone around the archway the iron staples which supported the gallows erected for public executions. Attached to the wall on either side of the narrow lane are the iron rings which carried the chains to keep back the gaping crowd.

9. The tower of St. Mary's church rising 174 feet in the air seems to block off the south end of Northgate Street. When the church was rebuilt after the disastrous fire of 1694 the tower was designed to rise from the western bay of the nave. The massive piers intended to support it showed signs of cracking and the tower had to be rebuilt over the street. Although it has been claimed in the past that Christopher Wren provided a plan for the tower, it is now generally believed that the design was that of Sir William Wilson.

Of the Norman church built in the 12th century only the crypt remains to-day. Nave and chancel were both rebuilt in the 14th century by the Beauchamps. Fortunately, although the nave was completely destroyed in the fire, most of the superb perpendicular choir survived, as did the alabaster table tomb of Thomas Beauchamp and his wife Katherine Mortimer. The choir vault with its brightly coloured bosses provides an excellent example of the flying ribs, so slender and yet so effective.

The nave was rebuilt in 1704 with aisles the same height, giving the church the feeling of vast, airy space. The poorest feature is the window tracery which is distinctly ugly. Similarly the tower is a curious mixture of Gothic, Renaissance and Baroque and is perhaps best viewed from a distance. Indeed it is a splendid landmark visible for many miles on all sides of the town.

Off the south transept is the magnificent perpendicular Beauchamp Chapel built between 1443 and 1464 according to the will of Richard Beauchamp, Earl of Warwick, who died at Rouen in 1439.

Born at Salwarpe Court in 1382, the son of Thomas Beauchamp II, godson of Richard II, Richard Beauchamp had the traditional upbringing of a knight of medieval chivalry. Inheriting his father's title and lands at 18, created Knight of the Bath, in 1403 he served the King against the rebellious Percies. When Henry IV married Joan of Navarre, Beauchamp was chosen as Queen's Champion in the tournament which was part of the wedding feast.

In 1408 he made a pilgrimage to Jerusalem, on the way challenging and defeating the Lombard champion in single combat, paying his vows at Rome, and finally hanging up his shield in the church of the Holy Sepulchre. Returning to Italy, he joined the company of the Teutonic knights in a punitive expedition against the infidel in Lithuania and Russia.

On his return to England in 1410 he entered the service of the Prince of Wales who was shortly to be crowned as Henry V. When the Hundred Years War was reopened, Richard Beauchamp was Captain of the bridgehead from Calais and for his service was admitted to the noble order of the Garter.

In 1415 he attended the great Church Council at Constance as the King's emissary. That august body deposed Pope John XXII and declared John Hus a heretic. Returning to Calais, Richard Beauchamp took charge of notable French prisoners whom he brought to England and to his deep regret he missed the great battle at Agincourt.

When the invasion of France was resumed in 1417 Beauchamp was given command of one of the three English armies. He captured Rouen and played a leading role in negotiating the Treaty of Troyes in 1420 and in arranging the marriage of Henry V and Katherine of France.

A short time later the dying King made Richard Beauchamp the guardian of the infant prince whom he eventually conducted to his coronation as Henry VI at Westminster.

In 1437, relieved of the charge of the young king, he returned to France as Lieut. General of the Realm of France and Governor of

Normandy. The role of persecutor of Joan of Arc which Shaw gives to Beauchamp in his play 'Saint Joan' was almost certainly that of John Duke of Bedford the King's brother.

Richard Beauchamp died in 1439 'full of Christianity' in the castle at Rouen. His body, in accordance with his will was brought by sea and land to Warwick to be laid eventually in the chantry tomb which he devised and which was completed in 1464.

The tall tomb chest of grey Purbeck marble is set in the middle of the chapel and the Earl's armed figure lies under a hooped herse or canopy intended to support a rich velvet pall which covered the figure except on Richard Beauchamp's obit day or on great feasts of the church.

Let into the polished verge of the tomb immediately below the effigy are narrow bronze strips which go twice round it and carry the Earl's epitaph in English. Here and there the words are separated by tiny bears and ragged staffs, the Earl of Warwick's emblems. At each corner of the tomb is a tall bronze rod to carry candles which illuminated the effigy when the pall was withdrawn. All sides of the tomb carry niches with elaborate canopies above and decorated panels beneath. The larger niches hold figures of mourners, the smaller ones have angels each holding a scoll inscribed 'Sit Deo laus et gloria, defunctis misericordia'.

The bronze effigy, probably one of the finest examples of the medieval metal worker's art, was originally gilded and is wearing a suit of armour, reproduced here in perfect detail, which was made by the finest armourers of Milan in the 15th century.

The noble face, although not a portrait, as it was produced fifteen years after Beauchamp's death, expresses the artist's idea of a worshipful, noble knight of the time. The slender elegant hands which are bare and raised in a most expressive hieratic gesture of prayer and adoration, are remarkably life-like.

The head rests on a tilting helmet which carries the crest of a swan's head and neck encircled by a coronet which was the emblem of the Bohun family, the common ancestors of both Richard Beauchamp and Henry V. The effigy also wears the Garter of which Thomas Beachamp, Richard's grandfather, was a founder member.

At the knight's feet are the muzzled bear, the Beachamp emblem, and the griffin, the badge of Richard Beauchamp's wife's family, the Despensers. The ends of the bronze bars of the herse have enamelled shields with the Earl's coat of arms and the Royal Arms of England which Beauchamp carried as the King's Viceroy in France.

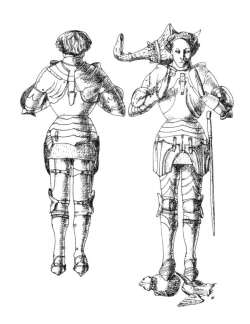

The tomb was the work of a Dorset stone mason, John Borde, the effigy and the mourners were designed by John Massingham, cast by William Austen and gilded by Bartholomew Lambspring.

On the south side of the Beauchamp tomb is that of Ambrose Dudley (died 1590), with another bronze effigy, and on the north side the over-exuberant, Renaissance monument of Robert Dudley, Earl of Leicester, (died 1588), and his third wife Lettice Knollys (died 1634). On the south wall below the sanctuary is the memorial to Robert Dudley (died 1554), 'the noble impe', Leicester's infant son.

Some steps on the north side of the chapel lead to a small chantry chapel, 15 feet long and 7 feet wide, which has tiny fan vaults with pendants and an altar with elaborate canopies above empty niches at either side. There is also an unusual wooden pillar piscina near the altar on the south side.

This chapel was probably used by the chantry priest to say the three daily masses for Richard Beauchamp which his will provided for, when the main chapel was not in use. From St. Mary's church walk along Old Square, past the Post Office on the right, to the Market Place.

10. Abbotsford is the eye-catching house of three storeys and five

bays in the grand style on the north side of the square. It was built in 1714 probably by Francis Smith for his father-in-law. It was refaced in 1963 and is used as offices by Warwickshire County Council. Its overall grace is undoubtedly marred by it being attached to the Shire Hall by a modern bridge.

11. The County Museum on the opposite side of the square was built in 1670 by another Warwickshire man, William Harlbutt, and was until 1879 open on the ground floor. It was used as a market hall. Unfortunately when the arches were filled the builder failed to copy the graceful style of the upper storey windows.

In the museum, where admission is free, there are good displays of local archaeology, history and natural history. Of special interest is a panoramic model of Warwick before the great fire of 1694 and the Sheldon Tapestry of 1588 which was given to the County Council by Courtaulds.

The Old Market House had many diverse uses through the years. Various trades were accommodated, one floor saw use as a leather hall and when the Shire Hall was being rebuilt in the 18th century, the Justices held their law sessions here.

In times of national alarm such as the Napoleonic Wars it was used to store arms and munitions, and the centre cell, which now houses the heating apparatus, served as the local jail known as the 'Black Hole'. Local debtors were confined upstairs in the caretaker's quarters. More pleasant uses include the provision of a stage for companies of strolling players and an arena for wild beast shows.

From the museum walk down Brook Street to

12. The Leycester Hospital on the north side of High Street and next to the West Gate. The timber-framed buildings standing on a terrace above the pavement of High Street were originally the headquarters of the combined guilds of the Holy Trinity and the Blessed Virgin and St. George and Martyr erected in the 14th century and enlarged in the 15th.

When the guilds were dissolved in 1546 the building was given to the Warwick burgesses who used it as a meeting place and also to house the grammar school. In 1571 when the town had fallen on bad times the burgesses sought the favour of Robert Dudley, Earl of Leicester. He offered help if the burgesses gave up the old guild hall where he proposed to establish a hospital or almshouse 'for such poor and impotent persons as shall be maimed or hurt in the service of the Queen or her heirs and successors'.

West Gate and Lord Lycester Hospital

The Leycester Hospital, set up in 1571, provided for a Master and twelve brethren to be chosen from the towns of Warwick, Stratford and Kenilworth, and from the villages of Wootton-under-Edge and Arlingham in Gloucestershire. To-day there are still a number of brethren in the Hospital, who on special occasions wear the black cloaks and the large Tudor hats with the original silver badges bearing the arms of Robert Dudley, Earl of Leicester.

The Hospital is arranged around a quadrangle and what was once the kitchen is now the Common Room of the Brethren and contains a collection of curios including a Saxon chair (?), a chair used by James I, and a wardrobe used at Kenilworth Castle by Elizabeth I. On the other side of the quadrangle the spacious lower hall has a stone floor and a fine collection of oak tie-beams, collar beams and queen posts support the roof. James I was entertained here in 1617. The upper hall which has been carefully restored was the actual Guildhall.

On the north side the Master's Lodging is a 19th century sham of plaster and paint masquerading as a timber-framed construction, and the whole effect is further marred by an excess of plaster bears.

From the terrace a stone stairway leads up to the chapel of St. James which is over the Westgate and which is an obligatory place of worship for the brethren every morning. This chapel founded in the early 12th century, was rebuilt in 1383 when the Warwick Guilds amalgamated and was much restored by Sir Gilbert Scott in 1863

13. *The West Gate dates from the early 12th century and remains today an impressive example of medieval building. The long, tunnel-like archway rises from the living outcrop of rock and runs along in a closely set pointed vault. On the west side the gate is Perpendicular in style and leads the eye up to the tower of the chapel of St. James above.*

14. *Directly opposite the Leycester Hospital on the south side of High Street and approached through a stone archway is the Friends' Meeting House, a simple brick building with decaying stone quoins which was built in 1695 to replace an earlier house destroyed in the Great Fire. Some of the original furniture has been preserved inside but the main interest lies in the quiet peaceful garden with its clipped yews. It is also the burial ground of the Quakers who perished for their faith in Warwick gaol.*

Walk along High Street towards the East Gate. At the corner of Jury Street and Castle Street is

15. *The former Court House which was built by Francis Smith between 1724 and 1728 and is probably the most attractive single building in Warwick. It has a wonderful air of dignity and authority without that pomposity that often mars civic buildings in provincial towns. The well-executed painted lead figure of Justice with the royal arms above and the former Warwick Corporation arms below set off the facade admirably. The restoration of the original open balustrade adds more interest to a delightful building.*

Francis Smith was born in 1672 near Wolverhampton the son of a bricklayer, and began his working life as an apprentice stone mason. The great fire of Warwick in 1694 gave him his opportunity. With his brother William he was employed in the building of St. Mary's church under the direction of the architect Sir William Wilson. In 1702 he made a good marriage with the daughter of a wealthy merchant and came to live in Warwick at No. 22 Northgate Street, now used by the County Education Office. Francis Smith was mayor of Warwick in 1713 and again in 1728. He died in 1738.

He is credited with the building of a number of fine houses apart form Abbotsford. One of the earliest is the handsome rectory at Hampton Lucy (see Walk 15). He also built Baginton Hall for

William Bromley the member for Oxford University whose house was totally destroyed in a fire in 1706. (See Walk 3). Unfortunately this house too was to suffer a similar fate in 1889.

Francis Smith probably designed Umberslade Hall, (now converted into luxury flats), for the Archer family who lived in a house in Jury Street, near the Lord Leycester Hotel, which was destroyed in 1694. He rebuilt much of Lady Katherine Leveson's Hospital at Temple Balsall and designed Sir Fulmar Skipwith's mansion at Monks Kirby.

Unfortunately there are no known records of these works. Apart from the former Court House in Warwick we know that Francis Smith did design the west front of Stoneleigh Abbey for Lord Leigh.

A final point to note about the Court House is the upstairs room, known as the ballroom, with its fluted Ionic pilasters and finely coved ceiling. It is a most handsome room which surely deserves much better decoration.

16. *On the west side of Castle Street is a splendid stone-built house of the early 18th century which has been carefully preserved. From 1826 No. 8 Castle Street was the dispensary for the Sick and Poor of Warwick and Neighbourhood.*

Notice that the capitals of the door and end pilasters are most curious, being fluted with finely carved ornamentations. To-day the house is a doctor's surgery and clinic.

17. *Thomas Oken's House stands on an island at the junction of Castle Street and Castle Lane. A fine timber-framed dwelling of the mid 16th century, it has been splendidly preserved as the home of one of Warwick's benefactors, a man of humble birth who became a prosperous mercer and merchant.*

In 1544 Thomas Oken was elected Master of the Guild of Holy Trinity and St. George and in 15th May 1545 formally received the charter from Henry VIII which provided for the setting up of the Corporation of Warwick. Oken is named as the Principal Burgess and in 1557 he was elected Bailiff or Mayor of Warwick. He died in 1573 and was buried in St. Mary's church. He left most of his wealth and possessions in trust for the relief of the poor of Warwick.

Early in the 19th century the Countess of Warwick set up a School of Industry for Girls in Oken's house. The girls dressed in 'brown stuff' and straw hats or bonnets and were taught reading, arithmetic, stocking knitting and flax spinning. They were employed from 8 a.m. to 6 p.m. in various kinds of sewing with two hours devoted to reading and religious instruction. The School of Industry

Caesar's Tower, Gate House, Barbican and Guy Tower

was closed in 1882 and to-day Thomas Oken's house in Warwick has gained international fame for its collection of almost one thousand old dolls. The Doll Museum is open to the public all the year round at specified hours.

Walk east along Castle Lane and turn right through the car park to enter

18. Warwick Castle. The Castle which according to Lord Torrington is 'the most perfect piece of castellated antiquity in the kingdom' was founded in 1068 at the behest of William the Conqueror whose successor conferred it on Henry de Newburgh.

That fortification was partly destroyed in 1264 by John Giffard the custodian of Kenilworth Castle and a supporter of Simon de Montfort. The castle on the south and east side was largely rebuilt by the Beauchamps in the 14th century. Thomas Beauchamp I completed the magnificent Caesar Tower 147 feet high in 1356, and his son Thomas Beauchamp II added the Guy Tower 128 feet high around 1380. The Bear and Clarence Towers on the northern or town side of the castle were added in the late 15th century.

In the 16th century Warwick Castle was held by the Dudley Family and when Robert Dudley's son was disinherited by the Court of Star Chamber (See Walk 3) and Ambrose Dudley 'the good Earl of Warwick' died without issues, James I sold the castle to Fulke Greville I in 1604.

Greville spent considerable money repairing and beautifying it so that in 1656 Dugdale described it as being 'not only of great strength but extraordinary delight; with most pleasant gardens, walks and thickets such as this part of England can hardly parallel'.

In 1759 Francis Greville became Earl of Warwick. Ten years earlier he had engaged Lancelot 'Capability' Brown to landscape the grounds. Brown planted thousands of trees, removed the old formal gardens and effectively shut off the town from any view of the river. In 1789 when the old bridge which led to the original south gate of the town was considered to be unsafe, the Earl persuaded Warwick Corporation to agree to the building of a new bridge 250 yards upstream if he was prepared to defray most of the cost. The Earl thus moved noisy traffic out of earshot of the castle and gained many acres of very valuable land. Warwick gained a beautiful single span bridge which to-day offers a most picturesque view of the castle. The designer of the bridge was another Warwick man — William Eborall.

The south range of state apartments which tower over the river were built at various times in the 17th, 18th and 19th centuries.

Madame Tussauds bought the Castle in 1978 and have made it a most popular attraction for Warwick's numerous visitors. More of the castle is now open and displays of arms and armour and splendid waxworks tableaux help to stimulate the imagination in recalling the past. Warwick Castle is open at specified hours every day except Christmas Day.

WALK 2
LEEK WOOTTON – GOODREST LODGE – MIDDLE WOODLOES – LEEK WOOTTON

O.S. Sheet 151 – 1:50,000 Stratford-Upon-Avon.
Distance 4 miles. Grid Ref. 290688.

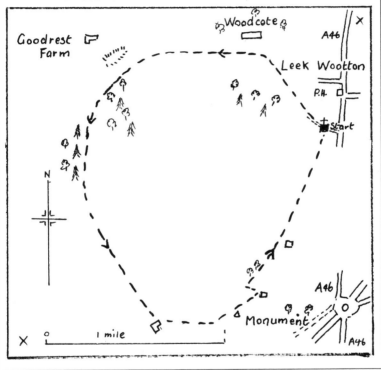

This is a pleasant short walk largely over pastures and across arable land where the farmer has left a good headland. The going is generally firm and there are splendid views of Warwick.

Approaching Leek Wootton on the A46 from Warwick go up a metalled lane on the left which leads to All Saints' church. Park tidily so as not to inconvenience either church-goers or residents, and walk up the lane past attractive renovated cottages on the right

31

and enter a narrow way-marked lane enclosed with tall, neatly trimmed holly bushes. Where the path divides, keep to the left to go over a stile into an arable field. Keep to the path alongside the hedge on the left, go over another stile and follow the direction of the arrow to go left along the edge of an arable field, with the wood on the left. The tall handsome house across the field on the right is Woodcote Hall built in the 19th century by John Gibson and now a police training establishment. It is on the site of Widecote Manor which appears in the Domesday Survey owned by Count de Meulan.

Over another stile keep on the same heading and at the end of the wood turn right and continue along the headland at the side of the arable to cross a tiny spinney, go through a hunting gate and follow the direction of the waymaker pointing left.

On the right the earthworks are all that remain of Goodrest Lodge which was probably used as a knights' lodge in the middle ages, and according to Dugdale, (Antiquities of Warwickshire), served the ladies of Warwick Castle as a quiet retreat during their 'lying in' times. It appears quite plainly on Saxton's map of 1576, and it is maintained that Elizabeth I stayed here on the way to Leicester's castle at Kenilworth in 1572. Behind the earthworks can be seen Goodrest Farm.

Across the grassy paddock go over a stile near the hedge on the left and continue across a large pasture keeping close to the hedge on the left. Go under power lines to reach a stile with a prominent Ministry of Defence notice on the right. Keep to the well-marked footpath through the wood and emerge by a huge sandstone outcrop to gain a superb view of Warwick dominated by the tower of St. Mary's Church. Continue to the right following the waymark signs to go through a gate and walk along the right hand edge of an arable field.

Climb a stile in the corner and keep on the same heading across a rough pasture observing the directions of the waymarkers around the edge of the field and turning 90 degrees left to reach a stile in the hedge leading into another arable field. Follow the path along the headland with the hedgerow on the left, go over another stile and climb straight across the next field, aiming for a mound directly ahead. Over a stile find a post bearing numerous waymarks. Keep to the right of the mound and the old hawthorn bush, and find a stile to the left of the house. This gives on to a narrow enclosed lane at the bottom of the garden of the attractive house. Come out onto a rough drive and turn left to walk past renovated cottages and continue on the same heading over a small arable field to reach a metal waymarked gate.

Continue now with the wire fence on the left, go under power lines, pass on the left of a trig point and go through a metal gate with a cottage on the right. Turn left and almost immediately left again and walk a little way up a lane to find a waymarked stile on the right. Over the stile go past the training jumps and continue walking on the headland on the left of an arable field. Over a stile in the corner cross a wooden bridge and continue straight across the next field aiming for a metal gate to the left of a large haybarn. Through the gate find a stile on the left and then immediately after, another stile on the right leading into a pasture. Climb the slope towards a mound with fir trees, keeping close to the hedge on the left. Walk through the stand of firs and follow the wire fence on the left to reach an unusual stile. Across a small paddock go over another stile, cross the lane, and through the kissing gate cross another paddock keeping the fence on the left. Through another kissing gate cross a drive and go through the churchyard to reach the starting lane.

To visit the Piers Gaveston monument from Warwick go along the A46 and at the large round about (grid reference 292676) turn left under the motorway and take the road to Leek Wootton. Immediately on the left find an obsolete road where you can park safely. From here you will find a well-marked footpath which leads up the slope and into the wood to the monument erected in 1821 in memory of Piers Gaveston. To-day it stands a gaunt, worn and gloomy reminder of those turbulent days. The inscription reads:

> 'In the hollow of this rock was beheaded (by barons lawless as himself) Piers Gaveston, Earl of Cornwall, the minion of a hateful king, in life and death a memorable instance of misrule.'

Most commendable inn fare is provided by the 'Anchor Inn' in the village.

Piers Gaveston, the son of a Gascon knight who had served and found favour with Edward I, was brought up as a foster brother with the young prince Edward at Langley. 'And when the king's son saw him he fell so much in love with him that he entered upon an enduring compact with him.' The prince was then 15 years old and the anonymous chronicler was writing 30 years later. Gaveston is described as a graceful, active youth, intelligent, nice in manners and skilled in arms.

In June 1306 we are told of a dreadful quarrel of the king and the prince when Edward I, like all the Plantagenets, a man of quick, violent temper, seized his son by the hair, knocked him to the ground and kicked him. The king it seems, suspected there was a homosexual relationship between the prince and his Gascon companion, and was determined to end it. Gaveston was to leave the country, although the prince made it clear that his affection for his 'beloved Perrot' was unabated. He went with him to Dover and showered him with valuable gifts.

Gaveston's exile was to be short-lived. On the 7th of July 1307 Edward I died and on the 6th of August Piers Gaveston was recalled, created Earl of Cornwall and granted all the castles, manors and estates that went with that rich, royal appanage. The English barons were plainly annoyed by the lavish favours granted to the Gascon upstart. 'The magnates of the land hated him because he alone found favour in the king's eyes and lorded it over them.' Moreover the more Edward's churchmen advisers counselled him to cool his ardour for Gaveston, 'the greater grew his love and tenderness towards Pier.' (Vita Edwardi Secundi — translated N. Denholm-Young)

In December 1307 to entertain the king, Gaveston promoted a grand tournament at his castle at Wallingford, where the Gascon knights scored a humiliating victory over the English nobles Hereford, Surrey and Arundel. Shortly afterwards, Gaveston was appointed regent during Edward's absence in France for his marriage to the princess Isabella. At the coronation Gaveston wore royal purple and was given the special privilege of carrying the crown of St. Edward in the procession. Confident of his influence over the besotted king, the favourite tactlessly displayed his power. He flaunted the jewels Edward showered on him, some of which Edward had received as part of his queen's dowry. Worst of all he made no secret of the fact that the king preferred his bed to that of the queen.

Gaveston's contempt for the crude, uncouth English nobles led to his undoing. He invented insulting nicknames for them. The king's cousin, the proud Thomas, Earl of Lancaster, he dubbed 'the play-actor' or 'the Fiddler'. The Earl of Pembroke he called 'Joseph the Jew', the Earl of Lincoln was 'burst-belly', Gloucester was 'Whoreson', and the Earl of Warwick who had rather a dark, swarthy complexion was called 'the Black Dog of Arden'.

In April 1308 the outraged barons met in council and threatened *civil war unless Gaveston was dismissed. The Archbishop declared that the favourite would be excommunicated unless his association with the king was ended. In June 1308 Gaveston was stripped of his titles and appointed the king's Lieutenant in Ireland. He was also provided with adequte manors and properties to allow him to continue his customary extravagant life style, and once more he was given a most lavish royal send off.*

He proved to be a most able administrator and was a successful lieutenant in Ireland where he exerted a considerable civilising influence on the uncouth society. He is remembered in Irish records as the first man in that country to use a fork at his meals. Meanwhile 'by gifts, promises and blandishments', Edward won over a good number of the nobles and having agreed to some reforms in the manner of government, he secured their permission to recall his favourite. At Christmas 1309 Edward, united with his 'beloved Perrot' spent pleasant days at Langley 'in long-wished-for sessions of daily and intimate conversation.'

Unfortunately Gaveston had not learned discretion in exile. He renewed his feud with the English nobles and most serious of all with the king's vicious, vindictive cousin, Thomas, Earl of Lancaster. The Lords Ordainers was formed led by Lancaster, to assist in the government of the country, but determined also to destroy Gaveston. In 1311 an ordinance demanded the favourite's perpetual banishment, and faced with the need for the support of the nobles in the renewed war with Scotland, Edward was forced to comply.

Despite the ordinance, in June 1312 Gaveston had returned to England and was immediately restored to his position and titles. His enemies were now bent on his destruction, and under the pretext of holding a series of tournaments, they raised an army and moved on the king and his favourite who were in the north. Edward fled to York hoping to raise royal forces there, Gaveston took refuge at Scarborough Castle, an unfortunate choice because it was not prepared for seige, and when Pembroke's forces surrounded it, Gaveston was compelled to sue for terms.

Pembroke agreed that the favourite should plead his case before Parliament and undertook to escort him safely to his castle at Wallingford. At Deddington, south of Banbury, Pembroke left Gaveston under guard to rest overnight at the rectory, while he visited his wife at Bampton nearby. The Earl of Warwick seized his opportunity to settle his score with the detested Gascon. In the early morning Gaveston was seized from his bed, dragged to the castle at

Warwick and flung into a dungeon like a common malefactor. The Earls of Lancaster, Hereford and Arundel, all Gaveston's bitter enemies, assembled at Warwick castle where he was condemned to death. He was taken to Blacklow Hill on the road between Warwick and Kenilworth and on the estates of Lancaster, and while the Earls watched from a distance he was brutally murdered. One soldier ran him through with a sword, another crudely hacked off his head which he presented to Lancaster. Four local cobblers carried the headless corpse to the Earl of Warwick who refused to accept it. Later Dominican monks sewed on the head and carried the body to the Dominican convent at Oxford.

For many months the king was inconsolable. The cruel, violent actions of Lancaster and his associates caused a general revulsion against them, and two years later Edward II made arrangements for an impressive funeral for his dear murdered friend 'Perrot'. Gaveston was buried with almost regal ceremony at Langley, attended by the king, the archbishop, four bishops, fourteen abbots, while funds were provided for masses for his soul in churches throughout the land.

Brave and accomplished, (he was a good linguist and a fine musician) Piers Gaveston was unfortunately inordinately ambitious and greedy, while his success with the king made him vain and recklessly imprudent. His pride, says one contemporary, would have been intolerable even in the king's son. 'But I firmly believe that had he borne himself discreetly and with deference towards the great lords of the land, he would not have found them opposed to him.'
(Chronicles of Edward I and II p.167)

Edward II never forgave his cousin for the murder of his favourite. In 1322 Thomas, Earl of Lancaster was defeated by Edward's army at Boroughbridge and on the 22nd of March, dressed as a penitent, mounted on a wretched, broken-down nag, jeered at and pelted with snowballs by a howling mob, his head was inexpertly hacked from his body by a common solider.

WALK 3
STONELEIGH – BAGINTON – STONELEIGH

O.S. Sheet No. 140. 1:50,000 Leicester and Coventry. Distances a.m. 2 miles, p.m. 2½ approx. Start Point and Car Parking, Church Lane, Stoneleigh. Grid Ref. 331726.

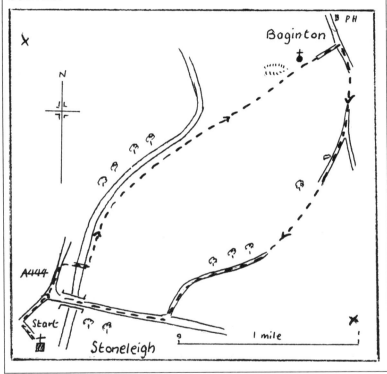

This is an attractive walk linking these two villages on the outskirts of Coventry. Stoneleigh still retains the atmosphere of an estate village whilst Baginton has important historical and archaeological associations. Both places are fortunate in possessing churches of great interest and elegance, widely different in character yet equally cherished. The going is flat following the meadows alongside the

Indian Balsam

little River Sowe in the morning and returning by a road and a quiet lane in the afternoon.

After parking and visiting the church, walk up Church Lane and turn right along the row of sandstone almshouses with their lattice windows and datestone of 1594, to the old forge beneath a chestnut tree. Go right, to the small triangular green, and then turn left with care up the Coventry Road.

Just beyond the garage and house is a finger post on the right pointing towards a brick pump house and bridge over the river sluices. Cross the bridge to a footbridge ahead and then go left along the hedgerow through a gate gap. Now follow the hedge on the right through the long field, eventually arriving at its end where, at a tall stepstile on the right, cross into the next field, which is often arable. Now continue with the hedge on the left and the Sowe on the other side of it. Clumps of tall pink balsam grow on the bank. Soon the sewage treatment plant comes into sight, then the nicely landscaped Coventry Golf Course. There is a stepstile beneath a tall oak and another riverside field. Follow the stream until a diversion to the right round a wired-off enclosure is necessary. Resume the former heading to another stepstile, and go on to a stile beneath another oak. Then comes a short pasture with trees on the left and then a field gate. Often a group of horses are grazing here, quite friendly and used to humans.

Now continue along a grassy track which follows a wire fence and goes gently uphill to a metal gate at the end of a line of hawthorns. Go left here over a stream and stepstile, then up the path past a house on the right to Baginton church. In the churchyard are the graves of Polish airmen who died whilst stationed at Baginton during the war. A short way off due west is a mound, now covered

Broom

with nettles, which was once the site of the Bagot castle.

After visiting the church, take the path from the west end (just behind the church), leading north (or right if facing away from it) to a black swing gate in the enclosing fence. This admits to an area once the site of Baginton Hall, which is still levelled but covered with brambles, broom and scrub. The Hall itself, home of the Bromleys, disappeared in the Sixties after standing in a ruinous state for some time. A path leads across this wilderness and turns gently left, eventually coming out down Hall Drive to Mill Hill and the main road. Turn left and go downhill to the 'Old Mill' on the right which we found to have an excellent choice of food and ale.

After refreshment, turn left out of the inn and walk up the village street, passing on the left the Lunt Roman fort which repays a visit. There are good views of the Coventry skyline in the same direction. Continue past the village stores and the Post Office with Bromleigh Villas on the left. Then pass on the right a triangular green which presumably once served the old village grouped round the church. Just past the Oak Inn and Coventry Airport take the right fork for 'Leamington 6½'. This is Stoneleigh Road. Follow it with care for about ½ mile to a junction where a signpost indicates 'Stoneleigh 1½' on the right. Go down this quiet lane which is lined with fine oaks but unfortunately is disfigured with litter of all sorts despite the desperate pleadings of several notices. At the junction with the road turn right and go down the hill towards Stoneleigh, crossing the river by the ancient bridge and returning to the church.

Stoneleigh

The church of St. Mary dates from the end of the 12th century when it consisted of a nave, chancel and west tower. The south aisle was added in the 14th century and the vestry in 1665 as a burial vault for the Leigh family. The splendid north chapel was built in the 19th cent. for the same purpose.

The Norman chancel arch is particularly eye-catching with crisp zigzag moulding in two of the three orders and with unusual responds which continue the moulding. Pellets decorate the outer order. The arcading in the chancel has been less happily restored and is altogether too heavy. The Norman font in the south aisle has arcading containing the 12 apostles, is in excellent condition and probably came from Maxstone Priory.

In the north-east corner of the chancel there is an elaborate monument in black and white marble attributed to Edward Marshall, in memory of Alice Duchess of Dudley and her eldest daughter Alicia. The monument has two recumbent female figures under a canopy and on either side an angel or cherub bearing a trumpet and holding back curtains. The Leigh coat of arms surmounts the monument.

Alice, the daughter of Lord Leigh, married in 1596 Robert Dudley, the son of the Earl of Leicester by his secret marriage to Lady Douglas Sheffield. Leicester later disavowed this marriage in order to marry Lady Lettice Knollys, the widow of the Earl of Essex, and when he died in 1588 his will left most of his estates to his brother Ambrose, Earl of Warwick, and only Kenilworth castle and its manors to his 'base' son Robert.

Having spent some years at Christ Church, Oxford, Robert Dudley equipped an expedition to the West Indies which explored the estuary of the Orinoco river. Returned to England, he married the daughter of Thomas Cavendish the navigator and when she died shortly afterwards, in 1596 he married Alice the daughter of Lord Leigh.

When James I became king in 1603, Star Chamber set aside Robert Dudley's claim to any of his father's estates and after a long dispute, in 1611 a forcible sale gave Kenilworth Castle to Prince Henry, the King's eldest son.

Feeling that he had been unjustly disinherited, Dudley left the country with his mistress, Elizabeth Southwell, a maid of honour to the queen. He eventually settled in Florence where he served Cosmo,

Duke of Tuscany as grand vizier or adviser on fortifications, finance, the making of roads and draining of marshes. He also dabbled in chemistry and invented a specific or healing powder which became widely known in Italy as 'pulvis comitis de Warwick' or Warwick Powder. His main interest however was navigation and his best known work on the subject, 'Del Arcano de Mare' in 6 volumes, was republished several times. He died in 1649 and was buried in the church of St. Pancras in Florence, now disused. The tomb bearing the familiar Bear and Ragged Staff is also the resting place of Elizabeth Southwell and their children.

Robert Dudley's true wife Alice died at Dudley House, St. Giles-in-the-Fields in 1699 at the age of 90, and her body was brought for burial at Stoneleigh.

The manor house in the village, north of the church, was built about the middle of the 16th century, and is an attractive two-storied, close-framed timber building which was originally L shaped, and had a wing added sometime in the 17th century. At the west end is a massive outside chimney, while the east front retains the ancient wattle and plaster panels, and has two of the original windows with splayed oak frames and mullions. Close to the A444 entrance to the village is a delightful row of ten almshouses dated 1594 and founded by Thomas and Dame Alice Leigh. Although extensively restored they have retained their original symmetrical lines.

Baginton

The church of St. John the Baptist is largely 13th century and contains a number of unusual and interesting features, such as a double aisle, a unique duplicated chancel arch which still retains traces of medieval painting, and an octagonal bell turret built into the east wall of the nave.

An exceptionally fine memorial brass on the south wall of the chancel is to William Bagot and his wife Margaret. With Green and Bushey, Bagot was a favourite and counsellor of Richard II, but was friendly enough with the King's rival Bolingbroke to be his host on the meditated trial by combat between Bolingbroke, Earl of Hereford, and Mowbray, Duke of Norfolk, to be held at Gosford Green, Coventry on the 16th of September, 1398.

Bolingbroke, we are told, rode out of the castle at Baginton, 'mounted on a white charger, or courser, barded with green and blue *velvet, embroidered sumptuously with swans and antelopes.' In the event the King forbad the contest and banished Bolingbroke from the kingdom.*

> *"Therefore, we banish you our territories, –*
> *You, cousin Hereford, upon pain of life,*
> *Till twice five summers have enrich'd our fields*
> *Shall not regreet out fair dominions,*
> *But tread the stranger paths of banishment."*
>
> *(Richard II, Act I, sc.iii)*

The following year Richard went to Ireland and William Bagot was appointed one of the 'souveraine's counsellors' left in charge of the kingdom. Bolingbroke took advantage of the King's absence to return from exile, overthrow the Council and seize the throne. Green and Bushey were executed, Bagot managed to escape, first to Chester, then to Ireland. He was finally taken, however, brought to trial charged with instigating the crimes of Richard II, sent to the Tower and released only to die at Baginton in 1407.

The Bagot brass is placed too high on the chancel wall to allow comfortable appreciation of its splendid detail. The knight appears fully clad in armour with a pointed basinet helmet to which the chain mail is attached by laces. The jupon covering the armour is embroidered with his coat of arms.

His wife rests her head on tessellated cushions, her hair hanging in two large plaits kept in place by an ornamental band. She wears a fur-lined mantle with buckles and a kirtle with an ornamental belt. At her feet lie two lap dogs with belled collars. Both the knight and the lady wear the Lancastrian collar of SS which suggests that Bagot was reconciled with Henry IV before his death. The whole is beautifully offset with black and red enamels, and is altogether a superb example of the 15th century engraver's art.

A little to the west of the church are rough earthworks, the remains of Bagot's castle. The basement of a rectangular 14th century building with the base of a stair turret on the west side are now completely hidden by grass, nettles and weeds. Apart from traces of the moat on the side, the outer defences have been totally obliterated.

The Repositorium Bromleyghorum An. Do. 1677 of oak panelling 7' high which once occupied most of the east end of the north aisle, in 1966 was resited at the west end of the aisle to provide a useful extra vestry. The Bromley coffin plates are now mounted on the side.

Baginton Hall, from a 19th century engraving

William Bromley bought Baginton manor in 1618. His son, another William, declared for Charles I in 1642 and according to the legend on the Bromley monument 'shared in the common calamity, sequestration and imprisonment, at last was obliged, till the happy Restoration delivered him, not to go beyond two miles from home without leave'.

This William Bromley married Ursula the daughter of Lord Leigh of Stoneleigh and the issue of that marriage, another William who attended Christ Church, Oxford and the Middle Temple, was elected M. P. for Warwickshire in 1688.

William Bromley soon became conspicuous among the 'high flyers' or High Church Tories as a most ardent advocate of the Bill against occasional conformity intended to embarrass the Whigs politically, and for his implacable opposition to Marlborough and the war against France. Nevertheless he was clearly highly respected for his devotion to the Queen and the Church of England and when in 1706 the family seat at Baginton was reduced to the ground by fire, intelligence of this calamity was conveyed to the owner while attending his duties in the House of Commons, and a considerable sum was immediately voted by Parliament towards a restoration of the structure. (Warwickshire − I. N. Brewer p.47).

Bromley was elected Speaker in 1710 and became Southern Secretary of State in 1713, but as a faithful servant of the Stuarts he refused office under George I and retired from politics on the death of Queen Anne in August 1714.

In 1727 he was appointed Recorder of Warwick, a position which he held until his death in 1732.

The fine house at Baginton where Queen Anne attended a house-warming and planted a cedar on the lawn in 1710 was destroyed by fire again in 1889 and today the site, just north of the church beyond the railings surrounding the churchyard, is waste land covered with brambles and willow herb, though the extent of it can be judged by the considerable flat area that has been almost completely smothered by rampant weeds.

The Lunt Fort at Baginton

This is an interesting experiment in reconstructing a Roman fort undertaken by archaeologists in the 60s and now administered by the City of Coventry Leisure Services for the benefit of scholars and the general public. It vividly brings to life the living conditions and daily routine of an army post which was probably a base depot for the campaigns against the Iceni, a powerful tribe of East Anglia who had revolted under their fearsome queen Boudicca in A.D. 60, captured and burned Colchester and London, and slain thousands of the hated Roman oppressors. After their inevitable defeat at a spot somewhere near High Cross, the Roman army under Suetonius Paulinus was kept in the field and sustained from camps such as the Lunt, which was also conveniently sited to protect the network of Roman roads criss-crossing the Midlands.

One of the great prizes which fell to the Romans after the final subjugation of the Iceni was a plentiful supply of horses which had formed part of the wealth of that tribe. It is highly probable that many of these animals were directed to the Lunt for breaking and training as cavalry mounts in the 'Gyrus', the grand ring which forms an impressive part of the fort's installations. It needs but little imagination to hear the crack of the trainer's whip and the neighing of the half-wild horses as they circled round it on the end of a long rein, and this impression is heightened by the sight of the realistic model of a cavalryman in the reconstructed granary nearby.

However, the Lunt was also a legionary camp, and the barracks for these hardened, highly-trained and splendidly-equipped troops are also on show with their outlines picked out in concrete. They were organised in centuries, groups of eighty men accommodated eight to a room with their commander, a centurion, quartered at the end of the block.

To the left, just inside the gate, is the commander's house, the 'praetorium', a complex building of considerable luxury with administrative and almost certainly bathing rooms attached, and further up the main road past the sanitary block and on the right is the 'principia' or H.Q. block comprising a small parade ground flanked by two long wings of general-purpose rooms closed off at the end by four more smaller rooms. These were offices with a 'sacellum' or shrine in the centre housing the legionnary standards. In the floor of the sacellum was sunk a pit to contain the unit's savings and valuables, a kind of strong room at the very heart of the fort permanently guarded by the standard bearers who were universally respected for their unswerving loyalty and integrity.

Every Roman fort was self-sufficient in food for long periods, as the staple diet of the army was cereals enlivened on occasion by vegetables, cheese and meat washed down with sour wine. The corn was stored in granaries and one of these has been reconstructed and is used as a museum. These 'horrea' were raised off the ground on stone pillars to prevent the damp causing the grain to deteriorate and were well-ventilated by louvres set in the walls. When in camp each legionary was allowed a ration of grain daily to cook and eat as he pleased either in the form of bread or a kind of porridge. There was no central means of cooking, and the men messed and slept in their small groups of eight.

The word 'Lunt' probably means a copse or wooded slope, and this is appropriate as the fort lies on an escarpment with gentle slopes now obscured by the houses of the village. The approach is along a grassy path dominated by the main entrance, a massive two-storey timber structure erected by the Royal Engineers in 1971. The timbers were placed in the original post holes and from the top level a good view of the camp and the surrounding country can be obtained. The gateway design was based on models carved on Trajan's column in Rome, the source of much valuable information about the Roman army. Timber, earth and turf were the materials used in the fortifications. The earth extracted and used to reinforce the layers of cut turf formed an almost indestructible rampart and also left behind a deep ditch which was in itself a formidable obstacle. When on the march, each night the legionaries were required to cut turf and build a small rampart round their temporary camp, and the timber forming the palisade was dismantled on breaking camp and carried off for use the next night. Permanent camps such as the Lunt intimidated the lightly-armed and *indisciplined Britons and as the country became increasingly Romanised towns often developed round them.*

The great days of the Lunt were from 60−80 A.D. with another period of importance in the 3rd century. Now it is an imposing reminder of Roman power and influence in that far-off era and can be visited daily, except Mondays and Thursdays from May 24 − September 28, or any day during the Coventry Holiday period.

WALK 4
KENILWORTH CASTLE – GOODREST FARM – LEEK WOOTTON – KENILWORTH CASTLE

O.S. Sheet Nos. 140 and 151. 1:50,000. Distances a.m. 4 p.m. 3½ Miles. Start Point and Car Park Kenilworth Castle (Brays). Grid Ref. 279720 – Sheet 140.

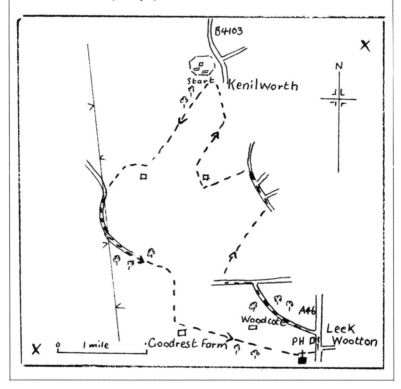

We offer a variety of walks in the environs of the castle, the usual long one which will occupy most of the day, and two shorter ones of about 4 miles enabling the visitor to enjoy a tour of the castle and a family stroll afterwards. Both castle car parks, the Brays and the Gatehouse, are used depending on the choice of walk. Also appended are a sketch map and notes on the castle. The going for all walks is flat, mainly over pasture and lane, with no difficult stretches.

For the long walk park as directed above and turn left away from the great hulk of the castle. Go left again up a shady lane which rises up to a gate and through it reaches another gate near an oak with a farm ahead. Go through this gate on the right, and walk along the edge of the fields until the ground begins to descend to a stile by yet another gate with yellow way markers. Here take direction gradually left across the long field and keep going till a ruined brick building comes into sight about half way along the hedge ahead. There is a stepstile and the way now goes right, following the hawthorn hedge. The walking is on soft grass and there is a superb view of the castle behind. The next hedge is predominantly ash and there is a large pool overhung with oaks. Straight ahead we find another stile and marker, and have our first glimpse of Fernhill Farm across the next field. Crossing amid the bleating flocks, we discover another pool on the left and arrive at a gate with a monkey puzzle tree near it. Over the stile is another gate by a tall ash, and then the way descends alongside the hedge as far as a tall upright post in the hedge on the right.

Ignore its blandishments to go right, and look for a path traversing left across the arable field in the direction of a power line pylon and an isolated oak. This brings us to a stile thoughtfully sheathed in plastic as protection against the wire, and after climbing it we find ourselves in the farm drive. Ahead is a white cottage where the Inchbrook goes beneath Rouncil Lane, or over it in wet weather, for there is a notice inviting motorists to try their brakes. The way now lies left, round the corner, under the power lines, past Roundshill Farm on the left and between the oaks and hawthorns of the lane for about 1 mile. Shady, and decked in may blossom the lane is a delight in early summer, and the drive to Goodrest Farm presently comes in on the right.

Go up this as far as the farm buildings and find a field gate on the left into the meadow which stretches down to an ash tree sometimes difficult to pick out against the wood ahead. Just before it on the right in the corner is a stile and waymarker from which there is a good view to the rear of Goodrest Farm, built in the 19th century near the site of Goodrest Lodge, a moated manor constructed by the second Thomas Beauchamp and used as a hunting lodge. Its name is interesting, deriving according to Dugdale from its function as a place of confinement during childbirth for the Countesses of

May blossom

Warwick. And Queen Elizabeth did sleep here in 1572 while on her way to Kenilworth to partake of Dudley's festivities there.

From the stile cross the little meadow alongside the wood noticing the hummocks on the right, the remains of the Lodge. Cross a small bridge to another stile on the left, then go through the trees to emerge into a large open field. The path now hugs the right hand edge and follows it round leftwards alongside a coniferous wood with the stone gabled Victorian mansion, now the County Constabulary H.Q., on the left. It blends in with the trees surrounding it, some of them no doubt planted when the Waller family was in residence. The manor of Woodcote was acquired by the Wise family in 1709 and the old house was pulled down, being replaced by the present one in 1861. Intermarriage with the Wallers brought it into the possession of the latter family whose last surviving member died in 1947, two years before the house became the Police H.Q.

The path marches on along the edge of the wood and gradually ascends to the top of a rise where it goes left for a few yards, then right over a stile and alongside the next field to pass over a stile on to a path which leads to the environs of Leek Wootton, a village which has some attractive stone houses but suffers from being bisected by the busy Warwick − Kenilworth road. At a thatched cottage we go straight on between tall hedges and past some pretty dwellings to meet the road, with the church, usually locked, on the right. Turn left past the Old Post House and the village shop, to seek refuge from the traffic in the 'Anchor Inn', where we have enjoyed many an excellent glass of ale, good food and conversation with mine host.

Some of the houses in the village are ancient timber-framed, and others are of interest for different reasons. One such is Wootton Court, dating from 1861 and just south of the village on the Warwick road, now a country club and sports centre. Just beyond it on a wooded knoll overlooking the by-pass is a stone cross on Blacklow Hill erected in memory of Piers Gaveston, detested favourite of Edward II, who was beheaded on this spot in 1312 by 'barons as lawless as himself', as the inscription says. The place is overgrown and sinister, as befits the deed and the man himself. (See Walk 2)

After lunch go left down Woodcote Lane just outside the inn, and follow it out of the village past the entrance to the Police H.Q. The lane is overhung by oaks and then young beeches and sycamores, allowing the sunlight to form pools of dappled shade. It passes over a mossy bridge and continues for about ½ mile to join Rouncil Lane at a T junction. Here go left for another ½ mile, and find an iron gate on the right near some oaks with a stile and yellow marker only a hundred yards or so from the entrance to Goodrest taken in the morning. The route now goes overland across the pasture to another stile by another oak. On the left and just visible is the jagged outline of the castle. Now the task is simply to follow the route across fields in the direction of the houses clearly visible and on nearing them to take the narrow passage which leads out on to Roundshill.

Go left down the pavement and soon Roundshill gives way to John of Gaunt Road. Tick off the house numbers till No. 81 is reached where another passage leads off left into the fields again. There is a farm ahead; passing under an oak make half left and uphill to the barn corner where is the inevitable stile, but round the corner past the gate. Climb the stile into the farm drive and just on the left is a gate. Go through it and skirt the garden, turning right at a gate with a blue marker. Pass in front of the farm over some hummocky ground to a small bridge, cross it, and make for a gate in to another field. Keep on the same heading crossing the field diagonally to arrive at the gate by which you had left the castle precincts earlier, and return to the car park.

A variation for part of the afternoon walk is possible. On reaching Rouncil Lane and arriving at the point where the footpath takes off to the right across the fields, look further up the lane and about 50 yards away just before the entrance to Goodrest is a finger-post with a blue arrow and the legend "2. Bridle Path to Castle". The path is well-beaten and follows the right-hand edge of four fields. In the fourth is a ditch on the left enclosed by wire, and on the right the red-brick farm. The way to the castle goes left as before, leaving the farm on the right.

Yet another variation for those wishing to combine a castle visit with a shorter cross-fields walk is to leave the car park as before, and on reaching the second gate beneath the oak go diagonally left, covering the last part of the main walk in reverse to Rouncil Lane. Return by going right, up the lane to the sign-post mentioned earlier and follow the directions across the fields on a parallel reverse course to the red-brick farm, where the return route to the car park is as for the main walk.

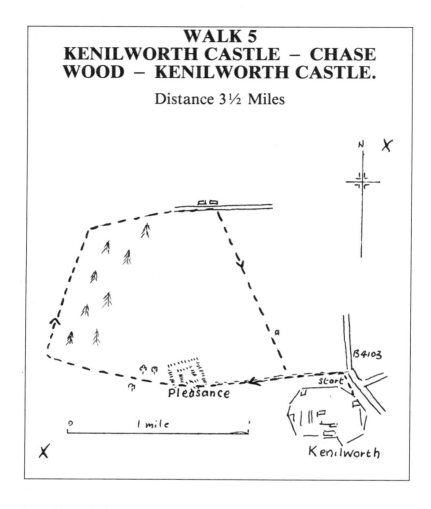

WALK 5
KENILWORTH CASTLE – CHASE WOOD – KENILWORTH CASTLE.

Distance 3½ Miles

For this walk it is convenient to use the Gatehouse car park. From this go left along Castle Road for about 50 yards to walk down Purlieu Lane, passing a charming timber-framed thatched cottage which seems to nestle close to the curtain wall.

Continue along Purlieu Lane for about half a mile and at the entrance to a farm yard fork right along a narrow overgrown path. Over a stepstile emerge into a rough pasture which is almost entirely given over to the extensive earthworks – all that remains of Henry V's pleasure-house known as 'the pleasaunce in the Marsh (en

Mareys)' which he built on the north bank of the great mere about ½ mile west of the castle. The building was dismantled in the reign of Henry VIII and the materials were used for a new building in the north-west angle of the inner court of the castle — 'a large great howse newly buylded of timber and tyelled wherein ys xij chambers above and belowe wyth chymneys and large wyndowes' — none of which has survived today.

Follow the track directly across the pasture which skirts the south side of the earthworks and reaches a waymarked stepstile in the top left-hand corner. Now cross a meadow keeping the hedgerow immediately on the left and over another stile follow a wide headland on the right of an arable field.

Over a plank bridge climb another stile and continue on the same heading with a ditch and a line of oaks on the right. The ditch and oaks now mark the original edge of the wood which is separated from the path by a wide arable field. Ahead on the skyline we can see Honiley Hall.

The path soon crosses a farm vehicle track. Turn right as indicated by the yellow arrow and follow the vehicle track along the edge of the wood to reach a T junction. Turn right and follow a quiet metalled road which skirts the edge of the wood which on this beautiful May morning was thickly carpeted with fragrant bluebells.

Continue past Keeper's Cottage and the drive to Pleasaunce Farm. Opposite a large red-brick house on the left, find on the right an antique stepstile and a footpath signpost to Kenilworth. Cross a wide pasture by a well-marked footpath with Kenilworth Castle now directly ahead. Over the next stile turn immediately left and go along the edge of the field, through a tiny spinney and then continue half right across a wide arable field.

Over yet another stile follow the footpath over two more arable fields to reach Purlieu Lane and the return to the Gatehouse car park.

Kenilworth Castle is arguably the finest secular structure in England which has survived without restoration from the Middle Ages. In the 13th century, standing on an extensive mound and enclosed on three sides by a wide lake, it was undoubtedly one of the most impressive and formidable military fortifications in all Europe.

It was founded about 1120 by Geoffrey de Clinton, chamberlain and treasurer of Henry I, Lion of Justice, and was probably the usual early Norman fortress of earth and timber. The massive keep which dominates the centre of the ruins today was erected by the second Geoffrey de Clinton about 1150 on the orders of Henry II who in 1164 placed it in the charge of the Sheriff of Warwickshire.

In 1199 Henry de Clinton surrendered all rights to the castle to King John who spent much time there and who built the outer curtain wall which he strengthened with a series of towers. His son Henry III completed the curtain wall and added the massive earthworks to protect the castle on the south-east.

In 1238 he granted the castle to Simon de Montfort who later took sides against the King and when the royal forces were defeated at Lewes in 1264 imprisoned Henry III's brother Richard and the young Prince Edward in the castle. After Earl Simon's defeat at Evesham in 1265 his supporters refused to surrender the castle to the King and it was besieged in 1266 from Easter until Christmas. When the rebels finally surrendered, Henry granted Kenilworth Castle to his second son Edmund Crouchback, Earl of Lancaster, but it was to return to the crown once more on the accession of Edward II, whose sad reign effectively ended here when he signed his abdication in the castle in 1327.

In 1361 it went once more to the House of Lancaster and John of Gaunt, son of Edward III, rebuilt the inner court and added the magnificent Great Hall with its sumptuous apartments. In 1399 John of Gaunt's son became King. Henry IV, Henry V and Henry VI all resided at Kenilworth from time to time. Henry V built a large hunting lodge in the park less than ½ mile west of the castle − The Pleasance.

In 1563 Elizabeth I granted it and the estates to her favourite Robert Dudley, Earl of Leicester and he undertook considerable alterations, modernising the 12th century keep and adding a new series of apartments to the Inner Court on the south side. He also built a gatehouse on the north side which was made the main entrance to the castle.

The Earl of Leicester entertained Queen Elizabeth and her court at Kenilworth four times between 1566 and 1575 and the lavish entertainments, celebrations and festivities of the 1575 visit are more admirably portrayed by Sir Walter Scott in his novel 'Kenilworth'.

When Leicester died in 1588 the claims of his base-born son were set aside by the court of Star Chamber and the castle was given to James I's eldest son Prince Henry (see notes in walk 3). Following Prince Henry's premature death it reverted to the Crown and as a result on the outbreak of the Civil War when Charles I failed to destroy the Parliamentary army at Edge Hill in October 1642, the castle was seized by Parliamentary forces. In 1649 it was rendered useless as a fortification by blowing out the north wall of the keep and draining the mere. Colonel Hawkesworth who had supervised the 'slighting' was allowed to buy the ruins in 1650 and he converted the Gatehouse into a residence.

At the Restoration the castle was given to Charles II's faithful supporter Lawrence Hyde whose son was created Lord Clarendon. It remained with the Clarendon family until 1937 when it was bought by Sir John Siddeley, later Lord Kenilworth, who handed it over to the Office of Works. Today it is in the care of the Dept. of the Environment and in 1958 to mark the 400th anniversary of Queen Elizabeth I's accession, Lord Kenilworth finally presented the splendid ruins to the town of Kenilworth. Today it is a place of brooding magnificence, majestic still, its mighty jagged pile overshadowing the town as it has done for centuries.

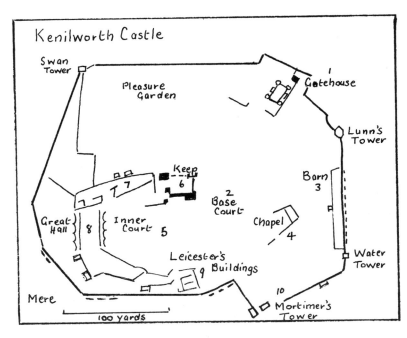

1. The Gatehouse, built by Leicester in 1570 was converted to a residence by Colonel Hawkesworth in 1650 and is now privately

owned and not open to the public. On the right a path leads to the Pleasure Garden laid out by Leicester.

2. *The Base Court is enclosed by a wall built by King John between 1203 and 1215, and on the left the massive circular bastion in the north east corner of the Court is known as Lunn's Tower and was partly demolished in 1649 when the castle was 'slighted'.*

3. *The Long Barn also built by Leicester in 1570 has recently undergone extensive restoration and possesses a splendid half-timbered upper floor.*

4. *Close by are the remains of the Chapel which was built by John of Gaunt at the end of the 14th century and which sadly was a victim of Leicester's alterations in the 16th century.*

5. *On the right the ground slopes quite steeply to the Inner Court which was originally separated from the Base Court by a moat which was filled in by Leicester. A small section to the east of the keep has been excavated to reveal the abutment of the drawbridge giving access to the inner gateway which stood at the angle of the keep where the portcullis groove and part of the springer for the gate arch can still be discerned.*

6. *The Keep originally 80 feet high and rectangular in plan is a most impressive, massive building with huge square turrets at each corner and strong pilasters supporting the walls between.*

It was built between 1155 and 1180 with walls 15 feet thick joining the turrets, whilst the battening which produces a series of narrow steps at the base, is no less than 20 feet thick.

In the Middle Ages the entrance which was in the first floor was reached by an external staircase on the west side. The upper door still remains in the wall near the north-west turret — the door at ground level gave access to the undercroft. Above were two floors each providing a single large room.

The keep was considerably altered by Leicester who made a new entrance through a postern in the north side, and enlarged all the windows except one on the east side. The north east turret has retained its original staircase and the north west turret still has the deep, noisome pit which was used as a latrine.

7. *On the west of the keep is a paved floor with drains and a number of fireplaces and ovens, all that remains of the kitchens. Adjacent is the Buttery with the base of the staircase which led up to the servery on the first floor of the keep.*

8. *The Great Hall on the west of the Inner Court was built by John of Gaunt about 1390 and was clearly once a magnificent chamber*

90 feet long and 45 wide reached by a wide staircase of which there are a few remains on the south side.

The entrance porch and doorway with its ornamental canopy and crisply carved foliage have survived although much weathered. Similarly the carved fireplace and finely traceried windows, especially the semi-octagonal oriel indicate what a splendid building this must have been in the late 14th century.

9. Leicester's Buildings built about 1570 seem rather flimsy after John of Gaunt's Great Hall. Most interesting are the holes in the walls which may suggest the building has been once the victim of gunfire. It is claimed they were made by Huguenots, refugees and silk weavers fleeing from France following the Revocation of the Edict of Nantes in 1685, who were accommodated in the castle before moving to more permanent quarters in Coventry, the holes being used to support their looms.

10. Finally, Mortimer's Tower built in the early 13th century was the main entrance to the castle before Leicester built the Gatehouse. The narrow passage was flanked by massive drum towers which housed the guard rooms. Each gate had a portcullis. Outside lay the causeway which damned the lake, and because of its length — 130 yards — it could be used as a tiltyard. The south end was protected by another series of towers and a barbican entrance which also controlled a sluice gate which could be opened to flood the area on the east side of the fortifications in times of emergency.

WALK 6
KNOWLE – BARSTON –
TEMPLE BALSALL – KNOWLE

O.S. Sheet No. 139 1:50,000. Birmingham. Distances a.m. 4½ Miles, p.m. 2½ approx. Start Point and Car Park Kixley Lane, Knowle. Grid Ref. 184767.

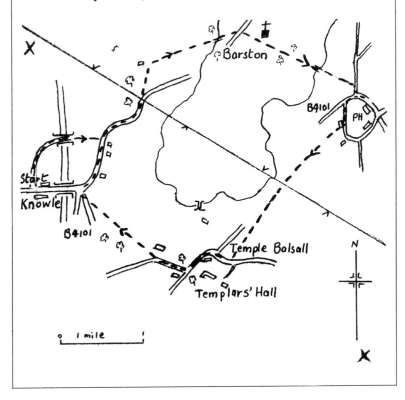

This is a pleasant walk over pasture and occasional plough with wide headlands through some of the area covered by the ancient Forest of Arden. It is not arduous, but can be muddy in winter. The scene is dotted by some splendid examples of timber framed buildings, as befits a former forest, and the 'Saracen's Head', the lunch-time inn, is an outstanding example of such a structure. The walk hinges round the complex of buildings at Temple Balsall which it would be difficult to beat for historic interest.

Knowle church and Gild Hall are worth a visit, after which turn left along the A4023 (recently re-numbered B4101) and then left again along Kixley Lane. At the end of this go over a hump-backed canal bridge and down a grassy path to climb a stile with a signpost. Bear slightly right, cross a plank bridge and reach another fence-stile bearing a signpost.

Walk along the edge of an arable field where the farmer has happily left a wide grassy headland, and keeping the hedge on the right reach Elvers Green Lane. Turn left past Elvers Green Farm on the right and continue along a quiet, twisting lane for about ½ mile to find a field path on the left boldly waymarked on the gate post with a yellow arrow in a green circle.

Cross a rough pasture keeping to the right of a stand of firs surrounding a pond, and continue with the hedge on the left. Where the way divides near an old barn on the left go straight ahead and cross over a high fence-stile. Turn half right and cross more rough pasture to a diagonal corner, the path goes between two tall trees and leads over another waymarked stile.

Bear slightly right to reach a footbridge over the river in the right-hand corner of the pasture. Over the bridge turn immediately left to reach a gate opening on to a lane. Cross the lane and climb the waymarked stile, then keeping slightly left climb a gentle grassy slope to reach a stile between two trees. Continue across another pasture with the hedge on the left, pass farm buildings, go over a concrete stepstile, and cross a small paddock to reach a signposted stile in the corner. A short narrow lane leads into the churchyard. Barston church is an attractive building erected in 1721. Cross the churchyard to a stile in the right-hand corner and go over a small paddock (on our visit occupied by an extremely somnolent piebald pony) to climb yet another sign-posted stile in the far corner on the left.

Go along a narrow farm-vehicle track, climb a stile and go half right across a pasture passing to the left of a stand of sycamores to reach a stile in the corner. Continue across an arable field alongside the hedge on the left. Go over another stile and keep the same heading with the hedge on the left. Over the next stile, turn right past a line of sadly decayed willows to reach a footbridge on the right.

Once over the bridge, climb a stile on the left and then turn immediately right to continue with the hedge and brook on the right.

Go over a broken stile in the right-hand corner and then half left to enter a close, overgrown lane which carries a small stream in places and could be rather wet in bad weather. Follow this path for 200–300 yards to emerge on to Barston Lane.

Turn right and after a few hundred yards join the B4101 (Balsall Street), then go left to the 'Saracen's Head' about 300 yards on the right. This superb timber-framed building which was in the manor of Temple Balsall, has been splendidly preserved and we found it provided excellent inn fare.

From the inn turn left and go down Magpie Lane which bends to the left, and on the right just before a barn go through a broken railing into a paddock. Keep straight ahead with the hedge on the left and reach a lane. Turn left and pass Balsall Farm House with a handsome black and white house ahead, to find a waymarked stile on the right. Bear slightly left avoiding a wet area and pass through a marked gateway. Continue on the same heading over wide, springy pasture to cross a footbridge. Keep in the same direction to reach a stile leading into an arable field. Follow the wide grass verge on the left, climb another high fence-stile, go left, then keep straight ahead over pasture once more, keeping the hedge on the left, passing a large pond, and going under power lines.

Climb yet another stile and continue on the familar heading with the hedge on the right. Temple Balsall now appears in view across the fields on the right. Reach the road and turn right to walk to it, passing the imposing Temple House, then turn left along a tarmac path flanked by a box hedge to walk past the Katherine Leveson Almshouses to the church.

After viewing follow the tarmac path over the brook and turn right through the waymarked gate along a path through the woods which soon emerges on to Temple Lane. Turn right then immediately left along the B4101 for about ¼ mile, passing 19th century Springfield House, now a school used by the City of Birmingham Education Department.

On the left of the school entrance where the road bends left, a path leads off to the right to cross a drive and a waymarked stile into an arable field. Continue ahead with the hedge on the right to the B4101 again. Turn right and after ¼ mile right again along the road signposted Barston. This leads back to Elvers Green Farm and to the footpath on the left which takes us back to Kixley Lane.

An alternative for the less energetic looking for an afternoon visit or a family outing which includes a short walk is to park near the cemetery gates in Temple Lane west of the church at grid ref. 204759. These gates form a war memorial to those of the parish who perished in both wars.

Go down Temple Lane towards the busy B4101 and just before the sharp corner take a woodland path on the right as far as a wooden gate from where there is a view of the church. Visit the complex of buildings and return to the wooden gate, and directly opposite is another which admits to a field. The indicated path follows the hedge and holly trees on the left, and soon there is a view of the buildings and a farm on that side. The grassy track meets a dirt pathway used by cattle and horses which can be muddy in the wet. This passes slightly to the left under power lines with a wire fence on the right and continues along the hedge line with open views on each side over the low-lying pastures.

Presently it comes to a stepstile and a footpath finger-post beneath some oaks at a junction of lanes with a small triangular green. Go right and continue up the lane for about ¼ mile past a pool and white house on the left to another T junction of lanes. Turn right as indicated Temple Balsall 1. This is Temple Lane and takes the walker easily back to the cemetery. Distance 1½ miles approx.

Temple Balsall and the Knights Templar

Balsall, meaning quiet pasture, is well suited to this remote place, once deep in the Forest of Arden, and today scarcely busier than when it was a preceptory of the Knights of the Temple of St. John of Jerusalem. It was they who founded the church which now, with the picturesque enclave of almshouses, forms the hamlet of Temple Balsall, a place best visited when the spring flowers are out.

The church is mainly of the decorated style, in red sandstone with a row of 78 heads, carved and set just below the roof overhang. They display all kinds of expression and fashion and probably represent the various ranks of the Templars. The interior is spacious, the roof supported by beams with Templar heads, the floor having different levels from west to east, to correspond with the different ranks of the Order, and there are no aisles or arches to clutter up the space needed by the company of solider-monks to accommodate all their panoplies and banners when they assembled here. The imagination must conjure up the scene when they were all assembled, for there is little now to remind us of their physical presence here, and the once proud Order has disappeared from the national scene as completely as the monasteries which once abounded in the land.

The term 'knight' is synonymous with the age of chivalry, roughly the 12th and 13th centuries, when Europe was struggling out of the chaos of the Dark Ages which followed the end of Roman rule. Civilisation and the rule of law were struggling to survive, and it was left to the church to fill the spriritual and moral vacuum. Church leaders believed that by taking young men of good families and training them in noble households, first as pages, then as esquires, and finally as knights, they could produce a breed of 'gentle' men pledged to protect the weak, and especially women, in a society which was crude and lawless. These knights were to be distinguished from the common herd by being mounted, and by fighting from horseback. The ideal of 'chivalry', essentially French in origin, came from the word 'chevalier', a horseman.

Hospitallier

These centuries were also the age of the pilgrimages to the newly-discovered church of the Holy Sepulchre at Jerusalem, which was under the rule of the heathen Saracens and later the infidel Turks. Though access to the church was permitted, the pilgrims were often subject to insult, danger and constant harassment on the journey and in Palestine. The affluent were taken and held to ransom, the weak treated barbarically and sometimes enslaved. The Crusades were designed to free Jerusalem and the holy places from the infidel, and in 1099 the city was captured and a Christian kingdom set up under a French knight, Baldwin, but the Christian hold was tenuous and the harassment of the pilgrims continued.

During the first Crusade the Order of the Hospitallers of St. John had been formed by an association of knights pledged to look after the sick, wounded and robbed pilgrims, and to provide hospitality in the form of shelter. The Order was well supported, it flourished and founded the church of St. John the Baptist in Jerusalem. The Order was simply a religious community of soldier-monks set up to care for the sick, and with no military functions at the beginning. The knights wore a simple black habit.

Templar

In 1118 a Burgundian knight, Hugh de Payen, with eight companions took vows of poverty, celibacy and obedience and dedicated themselves to the protection of pilgrims and to the redressing of wrongs and insults suffered by them at the hands of the infidel, by military means if necessary. The two Orders conformed exactly to the medieval notions of chivalry, and the pilgrimages afforded just the right conditions for practising them. King Baldwin gave the Orders a house inside the temple complex in Jerusalem, and hence came their title of Knights Templar.

Later the Templars received Papal blessing and adopted a form of the Cistercian monastic rule. Their uniform is described by Dugdale: 'On their heads they wore linen quoifs (like those used by Serjeants at Law) and red caps close over them: their bodies were habited in shirts of mail, and swords girde unto them with a broad belt; over all which, they had a white cloak, reaching to the ground, with a red cross on the left shoulder. Their beards were worn of great length.' (Antiquities of Warwickshire — p.576)

The east window in the Temple Balsall church shows on the left at the bottom a Templar in his white habit with a red cross on the shoulder and on the right a Hospitaller in his black habit with a white cross. It is from the Hospitallers that the Order of St. John Ambulance is derived.

By the middle of the 12th century the Order of the Templars had flourished to the extent that it had become lavishly endowed with properties throughout Western Europe. Individual houses, preceptories or commanderies were grouped into regions or 'langues', while the government of the Order remained highly centralised, all members owing direct obedience to the Grand Master. In England the Temple in London was the head commandery until its replacement by the New Temple in 1184. By the end of the 13th century there were 50 Templar houses in England, two serving as hospitals but the majority as centres for managing the Order's vast estates and for recruiting. The commanderies had few resident members, usually the commander or preceptor, a serjeant and a chaplain. Indeed there were only 165 Templars in England in 1308 when the revenues of the English Order amounted to almost £5,000, a huge sum for those days.

By reason of its unique connections with the Eastern Mediterranean the Order of the Knights Templar had become an important financial power in the course of the 13th century.

Its commanderies were all in correspondence with each other throughout Christian Europe and in the Near East. Their prestige, wealth and military power led rulers and nobles to use them as places of safe deposit or for the transmission of money to and from the Levant. In both England and France the Templars were acting as royal bankers and treasurers. In England they were often called before Parliament. In Palestine they were active as soldiers, always in the thick of the fight and establishing strongholds there and elsewhere.

Their centres of power in this country are usually indicated by the word 'Temple' in a place name, as in the Inner and Outer Temple. Balsall may be taken as an example of their development, as the hamlet and manor were presented to them in 1146 in the reign of Stephen by the Norman knight Roger de Mowbray, becoming a preceptory and steadily increasing in wealth and importance till the

64

suppression in 1312. Along with Balsall went other estates in Yorkshire and Lincolnshire. Roger de Mowbray himself fought in three Crusades, was eventually taken prisoner by the Turks, and ransomed by the Templars. He died in 1190 and was buried in Palestine.

The Templars' preceptory at Balsall was enclosed in a park with a hall, a chapel, lodging and domestic offices (pantry, buttery, bakehouse, brewhouse) all in one range of buildings. The Master had a suite of rooms and there was accommodation for knights and esquires (probably two) as well as six pensioners who were not members of the order. There were also a farm steward and a number of farm workers. Three chaplains and a deacon said daily Mass in the chapel. A charter was obtained from Henry III for a free market on Thursdays and two fairs a year.

'Preceptories' were so-called from the mandate given to the leader of the local branch by the Grand Master in Latin. This began with the words 'Praecipimus tibi', 'We order you'.

All went well until in 1187 the infidels under Saladin recaptured Jerusalem and one by one the strongholds of the knights fell until Christian influence in the Holy Land was almost non-existent. Although they were able to maintain themselves elsewhere their basic 'raison d'être' had gone and rather like the monasteries at a later date they began to outlive their usefulness. Their enormous wealth inevitably attracted blame for the failure of the crusades and criticism was fuelled by the behaviour of the Templars themselves. They had become arrogant and overweening, owing allegiance to neither King nor Bishop, and recognising only the Pope as suzerain. The complaints against them also contained more than a touch of envy and this became the real reason for their eventual suppression.

The King of France at this time was Philip the Fair, an unscrupulous monarch who was always in financial difficulties because of his extravagances and the anarchic state of tax collection in his kingdom. He coveted the wealth of the Templars, and was ready to adopt devious means to secure it. He had secured the appointment of a French Pope, Clement V, at Avignon, but there existed between them an atmosphere of mutual suspicion, rivalry, and where the Templars were concerned, collusion. Philip in 1309 prevailed upon Clement to summon the leaders of both the knightly orders before him after both King and Pope had allowed terrible rumours of alleged treachery, lust, immorality and irreligion to *circulate in Christendom. When the Pope had summoned the leaders to appear at Poitiers, Philip made public the charges which included the denial of Christ, requiring novices to the Order to spit on the Cross, and indulging in homosexual activities such as the ritual kissing of each other in obscene areas of the body. It is beyond credibility that an order with such a distinguished record of selfless service in Palestine should be deemed guilty of such transparent accusations, even given that it was provocative in its refusal to accept ordinary standards of conformity, and arrogant in claiming Papal protection in its overbearing behaviour. Its real crime was its wealth, and full confessions would be needed to make the charges stick.*

Philip however was ready. When James de Molay, the English Master of the Templars (his counterpart from the Hospitallers refused to come, claiming urgent business) landed in France with a large retinue and much treasure and was proceeding to his meeting with Clement, Philip suddenly arrested all the Templars in the country, put the leaders to torture, and in a short time secured complete confessions. The pathetic defence of the Templars, consisting of vain pleas for Papal intervention on their behalf, fell on deaf ears, for they had become the dupes in a power game between King and Pope. Some of the tortures were exceedingly brutal and need not be dwelled on, but they had the desired effect.

In England too, although the Templars were never as unpopular as in France, in 1308 Edward II followed Papal orders and had them arrested and their property seized, in spite of wide-spread amazement that the illustrious order should be thought capable of such misconduct. Special Commissioners, including Papal inquisitors, investigated the charges which included perversion, the practice of black magic, extortion and oppression. Of many of the charges they were innocent and confessions were obtained only under torture. Eight of the Balsall knights were implicated, and the punishment was disgrace and perpetual imprisonment in monasteries. After due deliberation Parliament decided that the Templar property should go to the Knights Hospitallers, themselves to be dissolved in 1540, but often the property was only obtained after long and costly litigation, and only after Edward II had used it to finance the war against Scotland and to reward his friends, includings his favourite Piers Gaveston.

It was a cruel, unworthy but perhaps inevitable end to an Order which had outlived its purpose.

The Katherine Leveson Almshouses

At the dissolution of the monasteries the manor of Balsall came eventually to Lady Katherine Leveson, daughter of Sir Robert and Lady Alicia Dudley, who in 1677 bequeathed the whole estate for the founding of a hospital 'as near the church as conveniently might be, for 20 poor persons, being widows, and poor women not married, of good lives and conversation, to be chosen out of the poor inhabitants of the said parish of Balsall and to have yearly the sum of £8 per annum, and also one gown of grey cloth, with the letter K.L. in blue cloth to be set upon the breast thereof, to be worn continually by them; and if they, or any of them refuse to wear the said gowns with the letters aforesaid, then to be put out, and others elected to their rooms'. (Dugdale, Warwickshire p.580).

The attractive brick quadrangle behind its iron grille celebrated its tricentenary in 1974 and the ladies are no longer required to wear the uniform. There is accommodation for four married couples.

Queen Elizabeth had given the property to her favourite Robert Dudley, and on his death it was acquired by the Sidneys in the person of Mary Sidney, Robert's sister. Robert's son at first tried to claim it in his own right but was not prepared to persevere, and though married to Alicia Leigh of Stoneleigh preferred to embark on an adventurous career in Italy with his mistress Elizabeth Southwell. Alicia however eventually forced the Sidneys to disgorge and after her the estate passed to her daughter Katherine who set up the almshouses.

Alicia and her daughter are commemorated by an elaborate monument in Stoneleigh church.

(see walk 3)

WALK 7
HAMPTON-IN-ARDEN – BARSTON – BERKSWELL – HAMPTON-IN-ARDEN

O.S. Sheet No. 139 1:50,000 Birmingham. Distances a.m. 5 miles, p.m. 2½ approx. Grid Ref. 203808.

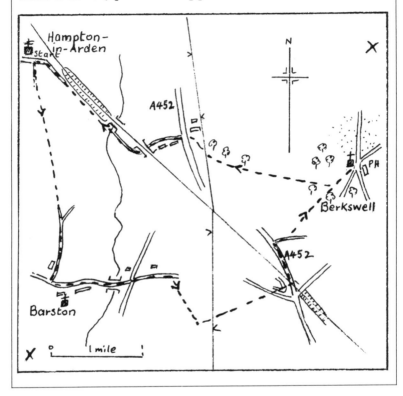

'Ay now am I in Arden, the more fool I; when I was at home, I was in a better place, but travellers must be content'. (Touchstone – As you like it. Act II Scene IV).

Sandwiched as it is between the sprawling conurbations of Birmingham and Coventry, Hampton-in-Arden today can scarcely be described as the sylvan arcadia of Shakespeare's play, yet the village still retains a certain charm and rural ambience.

It is a large village stretched along a hill slope surmounted by a

68

church and a number of timber-framed houses, of which Moat Farm immediately west of the church is the most impressive. The church, which was much restored about 100 years ago has a Norman nave and south arcade, a 13th century north arcade and a 15th century tower, an important landmark in the surrounding forest with its spire topping the trees, until 'by extraordinary violence of Lightening and Thunder, happening on St. Andrew's day at night, in the year 1643, it was cloven and fell to the ground, at which time the whole fabrick, with the tower, were torn in divers places'. (W. Dugdale – The Antiquities of Warwickshire p. 957).

This walk begins by crossing fields, often high with grain in summer, then there is a stretch of road through Barston and more field work to Balsall Common and Berkswell. The afternoon route traverses a park, skirts woods and goes up a lane as it returns to Hampton. It is mainly level but appropriate footwear is necessary, especially in winter.

Begin in Belle Terrace, a quiet cul de sac opposite the church. About 100 yards along the terrace on the left find a narrow path between the free-standing garages which leads over a stile into a grassy paddock. Go half right to another stile near a gate and continue in the same direction past a pond on the right, to go through a hedge gap. Continue keeping the hedge on the right to go over a stile on the right of a row of fir trees. Follow the well-marked path between the firs to come upon another stile in the corner. Now cross an arable field following a well-trodden track to reach a sturdy wooden footbridge over a stream.

Across the bridge climb a pasture to a stile in the hedgerow straight ahead and continue across another arable field, aiming for a fence-stile to the left of a solitary oak. Walk now with the wire fence on the left, go over a stile in a hedge and cross more ploughed land to pass between oak trees, heading for the top of a short rise and passing on the way two more oaks which mark the line of an ancient hedge, now no more.

From the top of the rise keep on the same heading with a thick hedgerow on the right. The path descends steadily to pass a ruinous Dutch barn on the right, to go over a stile and climb a green lane or farm vehicle track running between hedges. After a few hundred yards reach Oak Lane, turn right and go past houses, turning left when the lane joins the road at a telephone kiosk. Turn left into the tiny pretty village of Barston. Pass the 'Bull's Head' on the left and the neat red-brick church built in 1721 on the right.

Continue past the impressive 18th century Hall to cross the bridge over the River Blythe, constructed as it says on the plaque by public subscription in 1859. At the crossroads keep straight ahead to climb Wootton Lane and at the bend at the top of the slope. directly opposite the red-roofed house called 'The Trees', find a fence-stile carrying a yellow marker.

Continue now with the hedge on the left to go past a gas-pumping station and over another way-marked stile. Keep on the same heading. Ignore the waymarked sign on the fence on the left and cross another stile into a pasture. Go ahead to cross another way-marked stile and over more pasture going slightly half right to find a stile at the hedge junction. Continue with the hedge now on the right to reach a wide hedge gap and with farm buildings in sight about 200 yards ahead turn sharp left. Keeping the hedge on the left pass a grassy hollow with gorse bushes and young oaks.

Gorse

Carry on for a few hundred yards and when the hedge swings left follow the path which goes slightly right to find a waymarked hedge-gap. Through this turn right and after a few yards left with the barbed wire fence on the right. Pick your way through a clutter of farm machinery and turn right along a lane. After about 200 yards find an enclosed path around the bend on the left and just before No. 14. The path leads to the front car park of the 'George Inn' on the A452.

Turn left along the footpath beside the busy dual carriageway, cross the railway and take the road signposted to Berkswell on the right. After about 300 yards find a finger post on the left and go along an enclosed path and through a kissing gate into an arable field. Keep the hedge on the left and descend to the edge of a wood where a signpost directs left to Hampton and right to Balsall. Go through a metal kissing gate on the right and through a small spinney to reach a wooden causeway alongside a stream. At the end of the causeway cross a short paddock to enter the churchyard of St. John the Baptist church, Berkswell. From the church go left along Lavender Hall Lane to come upon the 'Bear', a well-preserved 16th century timber-framed house which provides a good variety of inn food and drink.

On leaving the 'Bear' return along Lavender Hall Lane, go through the churchyard and cross the paddock and wooden cause-way once more, go through the spinney and at the signpost to Hampton turn right across a well-marked path over rich pasture, with the lake and the impressive Hall on the right. Go through a small spinney and then across arable fields keeping the hedge on the right. The waymarked sign points right into the edge of a pine wood and after continuing for some distance on the left fringe of the wood the route passes a pool on the left and then crosses a stile to emerge on to a pasture. Keep on the same heading with the thick hedgerow on the left, passing a farm on the right and going over a stile into a lane near some cottages. The lane leads to the A452 once more. Cross and go along the shady Marsh Lane on the other side, passing houses on the left. Swing right alongside the railway to go over a packhorse bridge where the parapets were kept low to allow free passage of the packs slung over the mules' backs. Five sturdy arches support the bridge and on one pier can be discerned the base of an ancient wayside cross. The lane goes right, parallel to the railway embankment, and leads back to Hampton-in-Arden with its taxing slope up to the church.

A pleasing variation on this walk for winter or wet weather is to leave the car in Marsh Lane near Arden House (ref. 220803), cross the A452 with care, proceed left for a hundred yards or so and turn right down a lane (marked private road, which presumably means no vehicles.) The lane soon becomes unfenced on the left and passes a belt of trees and undergrowth. Pass the turn to Mercote Hill Farm and go straight on, following the lane as it swings first left towards more woodland and then veers right. A static caravan comes into view by the laneside, then the turn off to Park Farm, and soon afterwards the track is joined by Cornet's End Lane coming in from the left.

Opposite this junction is a pair of metal gates and the path goes through these and across the arable field to the far side. Here follow the hedgerow to the top right-hand corner of the field and then climb a marked fence, go past a pool on the left, and look for a stile which gives access to another arable field. Descend this with the hedge on the right and cross it at the bottom left to a stile. Then skirt the next field and find a path between a bungalow right and some cottages left, which brings you to the road. Turn right, and go down the road past the village hall to the crossroads in the village, near which is the 'Bear'. This walk is about 2½ miles of good going, and the afternoon can be spent in following the same route back to Marsh Lane as was previously described. It is less strenuous and allows time to enjoy the pleasures of village and church at Berkswell.

Hampton-in-Arden began as a Saxon settlement, probably in the late 7th century, on the high ground which runs south-west to Henley-in-Arden. The early English name Hean Tun, later Hontone meant in fact a settlement on a high place. The village also lay on the salt route from Droitwich to Coventry and today Salter's Lane leading out of the place indicates the road taken.

Although sited high above the adjacent wooded countryside it was surrounded on three sides by the river Blythe which often proved a serious obstacle to travellers. When in 1547 the King's Commissioners came to evaluate the assets of the church they could not reach 'the porche of the churche because of the great and dangerouse water wch in winter at every raine so rageth and overfloweth all over the country thereabout that neyther man nor beaste can pass without yminyment danger of peryshing'.

The ownership of the manor was frequently in the hands of the crown and at one time in the 17th century was part of the dowry of Charles I's French wife Henrietta Maria. The Prime Minister Sir Robert Peel bought the manor for his second son Frederick who made his home in Hampton from 1852 until his death in 1906. A successful lawyer, he held office under Lord Russell and later under Lord Palmerston, and was responsible for the large-scale alterations in the village church in 1879. He was also responsible for the timely restoration of a number of timber-framed and ruinous cottages in the village, although today the renovations do appear to be rather artificial.

Sir Frederick was above all conscious of his importance and would never allow anyone to precede him on the pathways leading to his house. As a railway commissioner he saw to it that trains stopped at the village, a piece of egotism for which Hampton commuters today are eternally grateful.

The church of St. Mary and St. Bartholomew with its splendid site on top of the hill is however only moderately interesting. The nave and south arcade are late Norman with the familiar massive piers, the capital of one being enriched with finely carved heads. The narrow chancel was rebuilt in 1879 and in the south wall in a recess has been incorporated the demi-figure of a man bearing a shield which was probably part of a 13th century monument and which appears rather grotesque in its present position. Near the priest's door is a heart shrine, presumably once containing the heart of a Crusader inside the leaden box, discovered when the head-moulding was being restored in the 19th century.

The east window has some fascination. Originally placed there in the 15th century it was restored by Sir Frederick Peel in 1903 in honour of his first wife Emily Elizabeth Shelley, the niece of the poet. At the top of the window Christ in glory is flanked by angels, the sun and the moon and fire and water. Beneath are four lights, three of which represent saints in varying postures, but the fourth displays, from the top down, the English poets Langland, Chaucer, Shakespeare, Milton, Dryden, Cowper and finally Shelley himself. No doubt the atheist and pamphleteer would be rather surprised to find himself thus commemorated in a church window.

Circling the poets is a scroll inscribed 'unto Him that sitteth on the throne and unto the Lamb be the blessing, the honour and the glory and the dominion for ever and ever'.

Other features of interest are the rood screen given by the second Lady Peel in honour of her husband, a small brass of Richard Brokes, bailiff of Hampton in 1450, and the remains of the stone benches along the aisle walls for the weak and infirm which have given rise to the saying 'the weakest go to the wall'.

A short exploration of the village, which is bisected by the B4102, reveals in Fentham Road behind the shops the original school splendidly Dickensian in appearance, and still serving the community as a public library. It has the inscription 'By the charity of George Fentham this scholl was erected in 1782'. According to the V.C.H. (vol.2, Schools), 'George Fentham of Birmingham, mercer, by will of 24 April 1690, gave annuity of £30, £20 of which was for a school master living in Hampton-in-Arden'. In 1833 the master's salary was £42.

St. John the Baptist Church, Berkswell, is one of the most striking and best loved churches in the Midlands. It is entered through a fine 16th century oak porch with quite delicately carved arcading on each side, and was quite commonly used for the celebration of weddings in earlier days. Above the porch is a timber-framed room with its original lead-lighted windows and fastenings, which was probably occupied by the priest or the sacristan, since it had until recently a fire place and brick chimney. Today it is used as a vestry and was for long used for village vestry or council meetings when the councillors sat on the benches around the walls.

The Crypt, Berskwell Church

The nave was first built about 1150 and two western bays have survived from that period. The chancel is later in the 12th century and has retained five superb Norman lancet windows at the east end. The south aisle dates from the 14th century and here the whole of the head of one window has been cut from a single piece of stone. There

74

is also a piscina in the wall which suggests that there was once an altar in this aisle. The north aisle, originally with the chancel late 12th century, was for some reason rebuilt in the 15th century.

Entered from a pew in the north aisle, we come upon the most interesting feature of the church, the superb crypt which runs under the eastern part of the nave and the whole of the chancel and is altogether an exceptionally fine example of Norman architecture for a parish church. The eastern part was built with the nave about 1150, the western late in the 12th century. Almost certainly this beautiful crypt replaced a much older Saxon crypt which may well have been the shrine of a Saxon saint.

John Leland writing about 1540 maintains that St. Milred, sometime Bishop of Worcester, who died in 772 was buried here, but there is no known record of this. Another theory is that a relic of St. Mildred, sometime abbess of Minister-in-Thanet, who died in 725, was brought here by King Ethelbald of Mercia who had a palace near Kenilworth, and was a relative of Mildred. Again sadly there is no known record. It is possible that Ethelbald was converted to Christianity and baptised at the well which today is on the south side of the church, and set up a shrine in the crypt which became a centre of pilgrimage in subsequent centuries. Certainly the narrow stairways north and south which led to and from the crypt through the thickness of the wall suggest that they were designed for the progress of pilgrims, except that the stairs are not worn so that Berkswell could not have been for long a popular site of pilgrimage. Certainly Dugdale who always had a keen eye for these things, makes no mention of a Berkswell shrine in his 'Antiquities of Warwickshire' published in 1656. If there ever was a Berkswell saint he was clearly forgotten by the 17th century.

Most likely the church, the crypt and its relics were destroyed in a Danish raid in the 9th or 10th centuries. Nevertheless the crypt is of singular interest and outstanding beauty today. Indeed the whole church is an architectural treasure house of which the village is justly proud, and although the threat of vandalism prevents it from being open every day, invariably at weekends there are friends of the church in attendance to admit visitors and point out its beauties.

The inn was formerly called the 'Bear and Ragged Staff', and is late 16thc. Opposite is another 16thc. timber-framed house. The guns outside the inn are from the Crimean War and in the museum is the account for a feast held to celebrate the end of the war.

The handsome manor has had a chequered history, having

belonged at different times to the Earls of Warwick and to John Dudley Earl of Leicester, but on his attainder it reverted to the Crown. Thereafter it passed through the ownership of the Marrow family, the Knightleys, the Eardley-Wilmots — but since 1888 or 1889 it has belonged to the Wheatleys, one of whom laid the foundation stone for the village hall.

From early times certain lands and premises within the manor were held by the churchwardens for the use of the church and the upkeep of the school. Some rents were directed to the relief of the poor and some cottages were inhabited without rent. Later some holdings were sold and the money invested, which together with private bequests have assisted church, school and poor alike. The village is well endowed with such charities.

Two other features are to be noted. The first is the well and the village stocks, and the second the little folk museum behind the almshouses, situated in the old nurse's house, itself a museum. This is improving with every visit, and is a commendable example of local initiative. At the moment it is open at weekends and is staffed by volunteers.

WALK 8
SOLIHULL – RAVENSHAW –
BERRY HALL – SOLIHULL

O.S. Sheet No. 139 1:50,000 Birmingham. Distance 4 miles approx. Start Municipal Car Park. Grid Ref. 159796.

There are pleasures in store for those who do not know Solihull, or think it merely an appendage of the great conurbation of the West Midlands. The town has a sharp identity of its own and many jewels in its crown, chief among them its church, school, park and the numerous timber-framed buildings in the High Street which bear testimony to the town's 13th century origin. The old and the new co-exist easily here, for the spacious shopping centre is but a stone's throw from the ancient Manor House, and the suburban homes of the affluent Birmingham business community are the modern counterparts of the commodious Edwardian and Victorian dwellings of the earlier industrialists who had made the village their residential centre. It is and always has been a developing and changing community whose history pre-dates and transcends that of its gigantic neighbour.

'Solihull' means miry, or muddy, hill, and on this forest eminence was built the first church in about 1220. Around it the settlement grew, absorbing both Ulverley and Longdon which are mentioned in Domesday. An influx of iron workers from Sussex, troubled by French raids, also swelled the population, and in 1242 the place was granted a market as a centre for agriculture and the manufacture of hunting weapons. The forest was gradually cleared and provided the timber for the early houses, so that when prosperity came to the area the essential elements of a successful community were already well established. The church was enlarged and beautified over the centuries until it became the present sumptuous building of red sandstone surmounted by a soaring spire. The dedication is unusually to the Saxon Archbishop of Canterbury St. Alphege, whom the Danes cruelly pelted to death with bones.

When the chancel was enlarged between 1270 and 1290 a two-storied chantry chapel to be dedicated to St. Alphege the martyred Archbishop was designed to take up most of the north side. The lower storey is entered through an ancient nail-studded door and by descending six steps. There is some doubt as to the original purpose of this splendidly vaulted undercroft. Was it built as a crypt for precious relics, a chapel to hold the holy sacrament, a sacristy, or simply to provide living quarters for the priest who served the chapel above?

The crypt or lower chapel with its groined ceiling is lit by four narrow single-light, trefoil-headed windows in the external walls. These windows were originally unglazed as can be seen from the rebates for wooden shutters and the vestiges of iron work to support the shutter hinges. Both window shutters and the door were secured by wooden bars from the inside.

Under the east window is an ancient stone altar with five consecration crosses to represent the five wounds of the crucified Christ. There is also an aumbry beneath the altar while the steps leading up to it are slabs of cannel or candle coal.

The upper or chantry chapel is approached by a raking stone staircase of eleven steps and through a doorway ingeniously corbelled into the chancel wall. This was probably the original chantry chapel of St. Alphege founded by the lord of the manor William de Odinsells in 1301. The east window which is by Burne-Jones also contains a few fragments of the grisaille glass which once filled all the windows of the chapel. On the south side of the chapel clear windows offer a most dramatic view of the fine chancel below.

The Greswolde family have been connected with the town since Henry VI appointed Thomas Greswolde custodian of the manor, and they built the Manor House in the High Street to confirm their status. In the 18th century they built Malvern Hall, and their coats of arms of two greyhounds appear frequently in the church. The Manor House and Malvern Hall are still serving the community, the first as a civic meeting place for societies, the second as a Girl's School. Other personalities with local affinities were the minor Warwickshire poets William Shenston and Richard Jago who attended the 18th century grammar school which is sometimes claimed to have been founded in the reign of Richard II.

The school almost engaged Dr. Samuel Johnson as Master in 1735, but sadly the interviewing body gave him an adverse report. 'All agree that he is an excellent scholar, and in that account deserves much better than to be Schoolmaster of Solihull. But then he has a character of being a very haughty, ill-natured gentleman and yet he has such a way of distorting his face (which though he cannot help) ye gentlemen think it may affect young lads; for these two reasons he is not approved on'. Nevertheless despite these *considerable handicaps, the good doctor did find employment at Market Bosworth Grammar School where, alas, he found a pedagogue's life 'as unvaried as the cuckoo's note'. (Six Counties' Walks' – P.II.) The present school stands in spacious surroundings on the Warwick Road.*

John de Feckenham, also previously encountered in 'Six Counties' Walks', was briefly priest at Solihull. He was a Tudor divine and ardent Catholic whose eventful life was spent in protecting those of his own faith and in maintaining miraculously both his religious principles and the respect of two sovereigns in an age of extreme bigotry and intolerance.

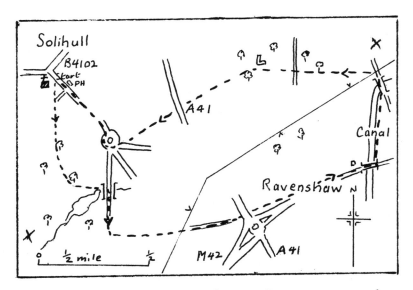

Solihull certainly repays a morning or afternoon tour, perhaps pleasantly rounded off with refreshment at the ancient 'George', in the square facing the church and famous for its bowling green, or at one of the many other hostelries. There is also an interesting walk of about four miles in the vicinity.

This starts from the church and square. With your back to the church turn right, opposite the 'George', and go down New Road. Where the road veers left go straight on along the path leading between Malvern Hall and the new flats, and enter the park. Turn right and cross the trim grass towards the tennis courts. Follow the tarmac path as it gradually swings left and arrives at a grill gate in the fence round the bird sanctuary where flamingoes, peacocks and pheasants are to be seen. Pass through it among the tall trees and shrubs to the gate at the other side.

Continue ahead to the lake and turn left to the road. Here go right and pass over the 13th century John de Sandall bridge across the Blythe. Sandall was Chancellor of England under Edward II. On the right is a former park entrance embellished with Doric columns in brick. Walk up the hill and past the elegant houses to Barston Lane on the left. Turn down this to the bypass and pass through the little facing gate. The path now goes left alongside the bypass to the corner. Now cross the bypass with extreme care, go right for about 20 yards on the other side, and then turn left down towards an electricity station. Leaving this on the left, continue along the enclosed path parallel with the M42. At the end of the path walk up the road to the canal bridge and turn left along the towpath.

Continue along the towpath past some moored barges towards the long low red-brick hospital with a central tower. The canal bends right to a bridge. Here leave the towpath, cross the bridge to the left, and at once turn left through a gate or over the stile. Walk up the track alongside an enclosed paddock on the right. Follow the wooden railings as they bend gently right and at the end of them climb the stepstile into the field. Cross to the next stile by a metal gate and enter the next field. Follow the hedge line on the right to another stile and gate beneath an oak. Then walk over the next field, go straight over the road and the field beyond towards the wood ahead which contains the remnants of Berry Hall.

The path goes along the side of the wood to reach a tree-stump stile leading into a pasture. Keep on the same heading and go over more stiles to go through a kissing-gate onto the main road. Cross the road to follow the well-trodden footpath opposite which leads once more to the by-pass.

Re-cross it with care to the footpath sign and continue to Oakley Wood Drive. Walk up this and along the tree-lined footpath on the left at the end to Hampton Lane, in reality a busy thoroughfare. Turn left and go down to the main road at the traffic lights with Solihull School Chapel on the right. Turn right up Warwick Road and fork left to pass the imposing Park gates and return to the church and square.

WALK 9
BEAUDESERT – IRELAND'S FARM – HENLEY-IN-ARDEN.

O.S. Sheet No. 151 1:50,000. Stratford-Upon-Avon.
Distance 4½ miles approx. Start and Car Park,
Beaudesert Lane. Grid Ref. 152660.

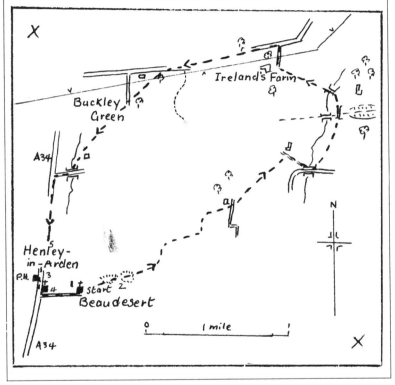

This is a delightful ramble, most of it over springy turf or along
quiet, leafy lanes, and offering pleasant views across a gently undulating, well-wooded countryside, a remnant of the Forest of
Arden.

The lane outside St. Nicholas' Church is a convenient start-point.
Go through the kissing gate at the end of the lane and climb the
steep, grassy mound, all that remains of Thurstan de Montfort's

81

imposing 12th century castle. Continue along the top of the mound, climbing in and out of deep entrenchments which probably mark the site of the dry moat surrounding the shell keep which stood on the higher ground furthest from the church. Now climb the path to the left-hand corner of the field, go under power lines and over a way-marked stile. Walk along the escarpment which is part of the Heart of England Way, for about a quarter of a mile to come upon a waymarked stile in the hedgerow on the right.

Over the stile bear half-left to cross a sheep pasture to another stile in the hedge. Turn left along an overgrown lane and after about a hundred yards where the path forks, turn right through a waymarked hunting gate. Go straight across an arable field and pass close to a neat, white cottage on the left to reach a tarmac drive. Across the drive find a hedge-gap and walk down a field keeping the hedgerow close on the left.

Climb a stile in the bottom corner, pass through a tiny spinney and keep on the same heading, with the hedge now on the right. Approaching the end of the field veer half-left to reach a tall stile in the hedge under a solitary hawthorn bush. Continue with the hedgerow on the right for a few hundred yards and go over another stile in a hedge immediately on the right of a stand of tall cypress trees near a farm. Pass a red-tiled house with a neat lawn on the left, go over a second stile and continue with the hedge on the right to join a farm drive, go through a gateway to reach a road. Ahead is a splendid view of countryside dotted with woods and coppices.

Turn left along the road to come upon the drive of Coppice Corner Farm on the left. Follow the winding drive for about a quarter of a mile to cross the bridge over a disused railway. Go over a cattle grid and find a waymarked stile close to a gate on the left. Now go straight down the springy pasture to reach a gate on the left of a power line pylon. Cross the concrete bridge over the stream, and across a small, grassy paddock go over a stile under a beautiful, massive oak. Carry on along the track which leads to Ireland's Farm perched on the hill ahead. At the farm entrance turn right to follow the drive until it enters a lane. Turn left along the leafy lane which winds pleasantly uphill and down dale. Continue past the T junction with Uplands House on the left, pass the neat farm with the weather-cock perched on the barn and just past the barn find the familiar yellow waymarker on a post near a kissing gate on the left. Following the direction of the arrow cross the field keeping the red-brick house on the right, to reach a stile in the hedge. Turn left along a rutted lane and after a few hundred yards come upon a waymarked stile on the right.

Go straight across the arable field with the power lines on the right, go through a hedge-gap and continue now half-left to reach a stile in the left corner of the field near some oaks. Walk with the hedge and ditch on the right, go over another stile, through a metal gate and cross a rough paddock with a white farmhouse on the left to reach a stile near a bridge over the Alne. Turn right and then left to walk along the footpath by the busy A34 into Henley-in-Arden.

1. St. Nicholas Church, Beaudesert is a particularly fine example of a Norman church built near the end of the 11th century. The rather squat tower was added at the west end of the nave in the 15th century and for some reason the north wall of the nave was moved inwards about 6 feet in the 16th century, and seems to encroach on the chancel respond on the north side.

The chancel walls have escaped restoration, and the east window we found especially attractive in its strong simplicity. It is decorated with zigzag and diaper carving inside and outside, and is supported by slender, round shafts springing from plain bases. On the wall on either side of the window are faint traces of medieval mural painting. The vaulted ceiling was erected in 1865 although the shafts and capitals supporting the groins belong to the original church.

The chancel arch is a perfect semi-circle of large span, decorated in elaborate detail with three receding orders of varied ornament, chevron, billet and zigzag, which have all been quite skilfully restored. The oak screen separating the chancel from the nave contains part of the 14th century rood screen. Inside the south door and on the east side is a remnant of an early Norman water stoup which was originally a globe with an opening in the front, but which now is sadly mutilated.

2. Beaudesert Castle. The high, grassy mound which extends east of the church almost to the ancient trackway known as Edge Lane, is all that remains of the castle built here by the Norman Thurstan de Montfort early in the 12th century.

Nearest the church is the outer bailey or base court, and separated by a deep trench which marks the site of the dry moat, is a higher, roughly circular mound which supported the shell keep of the Norman castle.

Peter de Montfort who became custodian of the castle in 1216, was to become the most powerful and most renowned of all the

Beaudesert de Montforts. Having served with Henry III on the expedition to Poitou in 1242, and accompanied Prince Edward to Spain for his marriage to Eleanor of Castile, he nevertheless joined the opposition to Henry III and was one of the twelve nobles chosen to represent the barons on the Council which formulated the Provisions of Oxford in 1258. In 1263 he threw in his lot with Simon de Montfort and was elected one of the Council of nine to govern the country. He was a member of the famous parliament of 1265 in which he served as Speaker, indeed he was the first Speaker of the English parliament. Peter de Montfort fought and died alongside Simon de Montfort at Evesham in 1265.

For taking up arms against the King his castle at Beaudesert was partly destroyed and the little town which had grown up near it, was burnt. The castle was rebuilt shortly afterwards but in 1309 the de Montfort estates passed to the Earl of Warwick, and the castle seems to have been allowed to fall into decay. There is no mention of it in the survey made at the end of the reign of Henry VIII in 1549, and William Dugdale writing in the middle of the 17th century states that there was not one stone standing on another.

3. The Gild Hall. The Gild of the Holy Trinity, St. John the Evangelist and St. John the Baptist may well have been founded in 1368 when there is mention of a chapel being built on the site although there is no written record of the gild itself before 1408. Like most medieval gilds it seems to have been rather like a benefit society, engaging in works of charity, observing religious services and saying masses for the souls of departed members. The gild enrolled both men and women and was governed by a Master elected annually when the accounts were audited. Its income came from entrance fees, contributions and gifts of land and properties as legacies. When the gild was dissolved in 1547 it held considerable properties not only in Henley and Beaudesert, but in Wootton Wawen, Lapworth, Tanworth, Beoley, Kinwarten, Preston Bagot, Claverdon, Ullenhall and Whitley.

The ancient home of the gild still stands next to the church of St. John on the north side, and is a timber-framed building dating from the mid 15th century. Following the dissolution of the gild it was rented as a dwelling house and by 1623 records show that it was 'very ruinous and decayed'. It subsequently was to serve many functions, part of the premises being at one time a tannery, a malthouse and finally a butcher's shop. In 1915 the building was extensively restored by W.J. Fieldhouse so that today very little of the original gild hall remains. The lower floor is now used as the public library, and the upper floor which was the gild hall is reached up a flight of stone steps from the courtyard in the rear of the building.

The hall is still an impressive chamber in which are preserved a few relics of the old gild — the brass mace bearing the arms of Henry VI, the truncheon of the constable of the court leet, and framed on the wall, the original charter granted by Henry VI in 1449, with the royal seal in green embossed wax. There is also a set of eleven large pewter dishes inscribed 'Henley 1677'.

As a seignorial manor after 1547, Henley was governed by a Court Leet and a Court Baron. The former dealt with petty offences and civil affairs and had powers to impose fines and mete out punishments. The Court Baron dealt with property matters, largely conveyancing and the transfer of land and property from one tenant to another. The two Courts met together twice a year and the officers were two bailiffs, a constable and his assistant, two ale-tasters, two chamberlains, two brook-lookers, two leather-sealers, two field-reeves and two affeerers.

When the gild hall was restored in 1915 the meetings of the ancient Courts were revived although the powers of the officers appointed were now purely nominal. Court Leet meetings have also been revived in Alcester, Stratford, Warwick, and Bromsgrove.

4. St. John's Church. Although records show that a chapel was built on the site in 1367 no trace of it has survived and the present edifice dates from the middle of the 15th century and is late perpendicular in style. The main structure is very much as it was in the 15th century although quite extensive restoration was carried out in the interior in 1865. The chapel of the gild was in the north aisle.

5. The Market Cross. The remains of the 15th century market cross stand at the corner north of the gild hall in what was once the market place. The much weathered shaft supported by iron braces, and three stone steps are all that remains today. The head which was allowed to decay and fall in ruins was a four-sided tabernacle with recessed niches containing the Rood, the Trinity, St. Peter and the Virgin. Once the centre of all the town's public activities, it was where all items of news and interest were proclaimed:

> *'These things indeed, you have articulated,*
> *Proclaimed at market crosses, read in churches.'*
>
> *(King Henry IV, Act V sc.i)*

The market cross was also the rallying point for all civic and religious processions, and before the Reformation was commonly used as a pulpit for open air preaching. Today the ancient market cross of Henley-in-Arden looks rather forlorn.

The main street of Henley-in-Arden, all of ¾ of a mile long, provides an extraordinary variety of styles of domestic architecture from the 15th century to the present day. Most of the buildings are 'listed' by the Department of the Environment as being worthy of historic or architectural interest. Moreover all the styles whether in timber and plaster, stone or brick were built with materials obtained locally so that they are in the spirit of the place, and human in scale; they all fit happily and harmoniously with their neighbours. It is most lamentable that the incessant traffic, much of it heavy, which thunders through the town along the A34, makes a leisurely appraisal of this delightful street virtually impossible. We hope that the opening of the M40 motorway will bring some relief to the town.

The 'White Swan' Hotel which stands across the street directly opposite the gild hall is an attractive timber-framed building from the late 16th century. It is made up of a middle block with a wide carriageway and gabled cross wings on each side. It is claimed that there was an inn on this site as early as 1350, but the earliest record which shows it as an inn is of 1608. In the early 19th century the 'White Swan' was extremely busy as a popular coaching hostelry when 22 coaches left Birmingham for London every day and 7 called here. From 1845 the inn served also as the local court house until the building of a new court in the rear of the police station in 1903. In the late Victorian period the inn was a favorite meeting place of the North Warwickshire Hounds until the coming of the motor car drove the hunt to find a quieter rendezvouse.

The 'Blue Bell' Inn which is some distance up the street north of the market cross is even earlier than the 'White Swan', being built in the late 15th century. Here we have an interesting L shaped plan with the northern end overhanging the steet. The gabled upper storey was clearly a 17th century addition.

Journeying to London following his Scottish tour in 1776, Dr. Johnson with his biographer James Boswell stayed overnight at Henley-in-Arden: 'We happened to lie this night at the Inn at Henley'. Although the honour has been claimed for the 'White Swan', there is no real evidence for the claim. There were 15 inns in the town at the time and the good doctor may have stayed at any one of them.

WALK 10
ALCESTER – WIXFORD – EXHALL
– OVERSLEY GREEN – ALCESTER

O.S. Sheet No. 150 1:50,000 Worcester and the Malverns. Distance 5½ miles. Start point and free Car Park in School Road. Grid Ref. 091575

This is a short walk which can be covered easily in a morning or afternoon's walking and which offers attractive views of the countryside across to the Malverns. Most of the walk is on good tracks or along quiet lanes, but the bridle path which skirts Oversley wood can be very muddy in wet weather.

Alcester is a most attractive small town of great antiquity and a leisurely walk around the centre is quite rewarding. There is some evidence of neolithic settlement and of almost continuous Roman occupation during the first and second centuries. Alcester was claimed to be 'the celebrated place called Alne' where a synod of the church was held in 709, when Ecgwin, Bishop of Worcester, consecrated the abbey at Evesham. The bishop seems to have had litle success in Alcester however, for while preaching to the wealthy, hard-hearted people, his words were drowned by the hammering of the many smiths in the place. He therefore invoked divine retribution, the town was swallowed in an earthquake and the site was given to the abbey of Evesham. (12th century Chronicle of Evesham – 24–27). John Rous the Warwick chantry priest in the 15th century ascribes a similar misfortune to Chad, who attempting to preach in Alcester, was driven out by the inhabitants and laid a curse on them. (Chronicle de Regibus Angliae). According to a recent publication, (Alcester – A History – G. Edward Saville –) the synod never took place and the episode was the invention of an 11th century monk.

In any case despite the curses of bishop and saint Alcester prospered, became a free borough in the reign of Henry I, sent two members to the parliament of 1275, and was granted a weekly market and an annual fair about the same time. Much woollen cloth was manufactured in the town and a linen industry was set up in Bleachfield Street in the 13th century. Later industries included the making of gloves, nails, guns and needles.

In the 18th century Alcester was a good market for grain, and malting was to become the town's most important industry after needle-making in the 19th century. In the great coaching era the town gained new importance from being on the main route from London to Holyhead, with the Swan Hotel as the principal coaching inn.

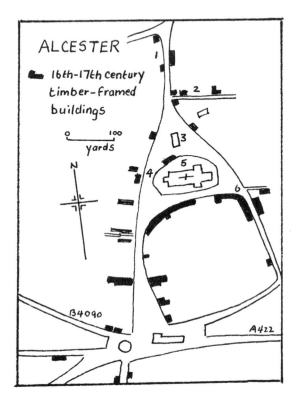

1. *Henley Street which was the site of the market from earliest times has a number of well-preserved timber-framed houses of the 16th and 17th centuries.*
2. *Meeting Lane also offers a number of timber-framed buildings. Here also is the red-brick meeting house which was licensed in 1736. Non-conformists first appeared in Alcester in the reign of Charles I and had to contend with the strong opposition of 'many great Papists of the neighbourhood and often the violence of unruly inhabitants much given to swearing, Drunkenness, and prophanation of the Sabbath, opening their shops, and selling Wares*

(especially Meat) publickly', so as to earn the town the name of 'Drunken Alcester'.

Despite such formidable obstacles, non-conformity gained ground in the town so that by the early 19th century separate churches had been formed from the Baptist congregation in Meeting Lane, in Henley-in-Arden in 1803 and at Astwood Bank in 1813.
3. The Market House, a two-storied building erected in 1618, was a gift to the town from Sir Fulke Greville, Lord of the Manor. Originally it was intended to be built all in stone, but this must have proved too costly, and the upper storey was not completed in timber until 1641. The lower storey, originally an open stone colonnade where the covered market was held, was filled in in 1873. A plaque on the wall informs us that the building was bought from the Marquis of Hertford in 1919 to serve as a war memorial.
4. Butter Street is especially attractive, a short, narrow passage to the right of the Market House, all that remains of a circle of shops

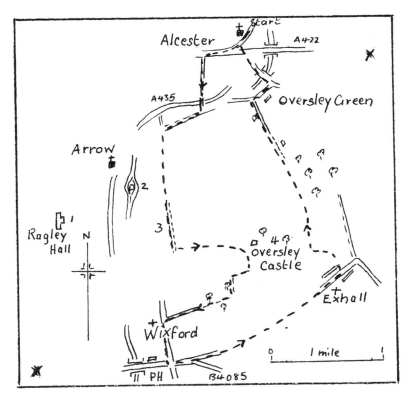

and houses which once enclosed the churchyard and was known as Shop Row. Churchill House at the junction of Henley Street and Butter Street has a red brick front of 1688 and some fascinating carved friezes on the main wooden cornice.

5. *St. Nicholas Church.*

6. *Malt Mill Lane.* 'The Old Malt House' at the corner of Church Street and Malt Mill Lane dates from around 1500 and is the oldest house in the town. The timber frame is very close-set and the tie beams seem unusually heavy. One of the attractive features of Alcester is the ease with which buildings of all epochs and styles — medieval, Tudor, Georgian, Regency, Victorian — rest cheek by jowl with one another, without any harsh clashes or tasteless intrusions on its architectural harmony.

In Malt Mill Lane, at the entrance to Colebrook Close, a plaque on the wall tells us that the restoration of the surrounding timber-framed houses was begun in 1972 and completed in 1975 by Stratford-upon-Avon District Council, a most commendable piece of local government enterprise. The lane now looks much as it must have done centuries ago, apart perhaps from the roofs and through the entry on the left is the most pleasant complex of sheltered accommodation grouped around a green. We can walk through this and, from the end of Malt Mill Lane, enjoy the quiet prospect of the timber-framed houses at the top, whose oak beams are happily un-marred by artificial colouring.

From the car park walk down Henley Street, past the church and along High Street to emerge on the A422 opposite the Swan Hotel. Walk along Bleachfield Street which ends in an unmade lane with a bridge over the river Arrow. Continue through a caravan park and turn right into a metalled lane. At the first bend go through a waymarked metal gate on the left and walk along the edge of an arable field with the hedge on the left.

To the right, topping a gentle slope across the river can be seen the impressive east front of Ragley Hall (1), and below the house on the riverside the ancient Arrow Mill. (2). The way now follows the Roman Ryknield Street, (3) and climbs gently through a spinney to reach a junction of farm tracks near a dutch barn on the right. Follow the direction of the waymarker, go left and climb steadily towards the dominant mound known as Oversley Castle. (4). The mound with its stand of sturdy oaks commands extensive all-round views.

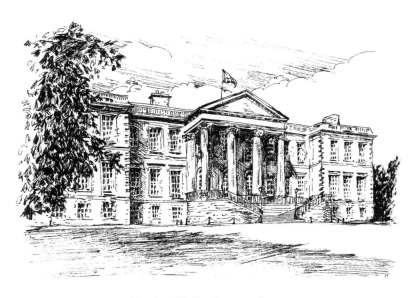

Ragley Hall, the east front

The way swings right, continues to climb for a short distance and then drops down through a splendid avenue of chestnut, birch, poplar and laburnum, best seen late in May when the bright yellow blossoms, falling in cascades from the branches, cheer us all the way to Wixford church. (5). From the church continue to the left to reach the B4085, turn right and walk through the village to the 'Fish Inn' by the river. Shakespeare once drank here, it is dubiously claimed, but the food, drink and surroundings are nevertheless very good.

After refreshments retrace steps to the road junction at the 'Three Horse Shoes' and proceed left along the narrow lane signposted to Exhall. (6). The church stands on the slope on the right; on the left the village notice board and a footpath sign pointing up to the cricket field and a hilly sheep pasture. Keep to the left of the cricket square, find a fence stile in the hedge on the left, then climb half-right up the slope to reach a high fence stile in the right-hand corner of the field. Over another stile walk along the edge of an arable field with the mound of Oversley Castle standing out boldly across the field on the left.

At the bottom of the field, follow the familiar waymark which points straight ahead along a bridle path, much churned up by horses, which skirts the edge of Oversley Wood. This soon emerges among the houses of Oversley Green, becomes a road which descends past neat, thatched cottages, swings first right then almost immediately left to cross the river Alne by a fine bridge built in 1600. Cross the busy A422 and follow the path over the green which leads to Gas House Lane and Malt Mill Lane.

1. Ragley Hall was built between 1679 and 1683 for Edward Seymour, Earl of Conway. The architect was Robert Hook, scientist and curator of the Royal Society and Ragley is the only surviving example of his architectural work. In 1750 James Gibbs made improvements to the interior, most notably adding the splendid Baroque hall with its delicate rococo decoration. 'Capability' Brown laid out the gardens at the same period. James Wyatt added the striking portico of the east front about 1780.

Ragley Hall is open to the public:
April to the end of September daily, except
Monday and Friday.

2. Arrow Mill, now a fashionable restaurant, was mentioned in the Domesday Survey of 1086, and was still grinding corn a couple of decades ago. Hard by among buttercup strewn meadows is Arrow church, burial place of the Seymours, Marquesses of Hertford, which with its old rectory forms a delightful corner of rural England.
3. Ryknield Street ran from the Fosse Way at Bourton-on-the-Water to Letocetum near Lichfield.
4. Oversley Castle was a folly or 'gingerbread castle' raised in the late 18th century to satisfy a whim of the Prince Regent, who was a close friend of the Marquess and, so rumour had it, an even more intimate friend of the beautiful but aging Marchioness. On his first visit to Ragley Hall in 1796, the Prince Regent suggested that the prospect of the house would be much enhanced with the addition of a romantic ruin.
5. Wixford church. The church of St. Milburga at Wixford is kept locked, but the key should be available at the nearby cottage. The church is notable for the south chapel which was added in the 14th century by Thomas de Cruwe, Lord of the Manor. It contains the low altar tomb of grey marble upon which probably the life size effigies of Thomas and his wife Juliana, finished in splendid detail, are to be seen in all their glory. The man is in full plate armour of the

period; his wife wearing a head-dress and veil, a close kirtle with buttoned sleeves and cuffs. Her mantle, open down the front, is held together with tasselled cords and rings.

Sir Thomas was attorney to the Countess of Warwick, consort of the Kingmaker, which explains the presence of the Warwick arms on the tomb. Immediately outside the church is an immense yew tree, whose outspread branches now require strong supports. In 1669 Wixford parishioners protested against the rector's threats to have the ancient tree cut down, insisting 'the like thereof is not to be found in all the diocese'. (Highways and Byways in Shakespeare's Country — W. Hutton. p.243.) In 1730 the then rector, Dr. Thomas, gave its height as 53 feet and its circumference as 18 feet 3 inches. The village was known in popular doggerel as 'Papist Wixford' because of the strong influence there of the Throckmortons of Coughton Court. The Wixford Manor was in their possession from 1562 to 1919, and they maintained the almshouses in the village as well as reserving the south chapel for the saying of masses for the souls of Throckmortons departed.

WALK 11
ALCESTER – COUGHTON COURT – NEW END – ALCESTER.

O.S. Sheet No. 150 1:50,000 Worcester and the Malverns. Distances a.m. 4½ miles, p.m. 3 miles. Start point and Car Park in School Road. Grid Ref. 091575.

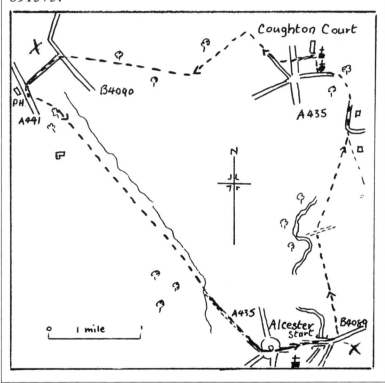

The morning route leaves the car park and follows the river Arrow northward to Coughton Court, a delightful house with a fascinating past. The route is flat and easy and after passing through the village of Coughton rises through Coughton Park woods to give good views over Studley before reaching the 'Nevill Arms' at the junction of the B4090 and the A441. In the afternoon there is a descent to Alcester

94

Park Farm and then a long, level return through arable fields alongside the Spittle Brook, with obviously danger of mud in wet conditions, but there are no really arduous stretches.

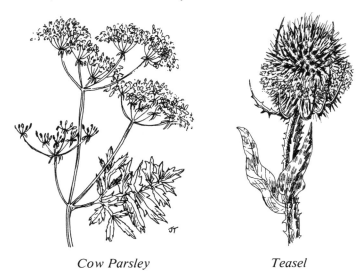

Cow Parsley   Teasel

On leaving the car park turn left, cross Gunnings bridge, and just past the Greig Sports Hall on the left in Kinwarton Road take the footpath which in season is overhung with may and cow-parsley. It crosses a road with the River Arrow on the left and a school on the right. At a junction of paths go right under a huge oak and enter the playing field. Keep the hedge and school on the right and continue along the hedge line at the end of the field under the oaks. Here the track goes first left and then bends right with the river to go past a small weir. The Arrow flows quite quickly over an occasional shingle or pebble shallow and has a variety of vegetation and birds on its banks; Cross a bridge and go right over an old railway track, then left following the river through a market garden area. Follow the bank left again over a stile and alongside an arable field then cross two stiles beneath oaks with young trees on the right. Here are clumps of teasel and comfrey. Soon on the left bank a group of white houses comes into sight, then an industrial building. Pass through a gate into an arable field. The river runs over a weir, then over a shingle bank. Continue along the field edge and go left at a red house to a lane at a stile. Go left down the lane to the handsome mill house called Millford, and left again just past it over a small bridge into a pasture. Cross this to a metal gate and walk over the next field with a church on the right to a white signpost for Coughton Court. Go up the drive past the two churches to the house.

Pause to admire the imposing facade before turning left down the drive to the main road. Cross straight over it and continue down the lane past Coughton school. The pleasant road passes over a bridge with a dry moat system on the left. It is overhung with oaks and hawthorn. On reaching a wood on the left take the path which skirts it with wooden posts on the left of the track. Continue through a hedge gap and along the wood side. The way eventually swings right, through the wood, and goes up a wide ride rising gently to a belt of conifers. Beyond this it passes through a patch of scrub with Studley visible to the right and then descends down to the road junction. Continue up the hill on the B4090, going left at the top to the 'Nevill Arms', warmly recommended for its food and drink.

After refreshment cross the road and go right to a stile on the left with a footpath sign indicating 'Alcester Heath'. Cross into a short field with another stile. Climb it and pass through a patch of scrub to another stile into a field. Half-way along is a fence and gate on the right. Enter the wood and go half left over an awkward stile into a field. The way goes down the line of trees to two ruinous barns on the right. Come off the slope half right to a gate in the corner and cross the arable field to a fence at a farm track.

Here the way has been diverted left, indicated by a black arrow, down the track to a small barn. Pass through the gate on the right indicated by the arrow and follow the hedge down to the field bottom. Here go right along the field edge with a wire fence and stream, the Spittle Brook, on the left. Go right at the field end for about twenty yards to a stile on the left with a black arrow. Cross and again follow the hedge line on the left and the brook. Cross the stream at a farm bridge and on the other side go left to a ruined barn. The whole scene here is one of intensive cultivation, every field being under the plough. It is rape at the moment of writing.

There is a gate on the right, and through it go left again along the hedge to another with a green footpath sign. Pass left through it again and then right to the brook, continuing by it until a house appears on the right. Then go left and right through another gate gap, again indicated, and cross the brook, staying on the other side until swinging right to a farm track. Turn left down this to the road leading up to Cold Comfort Farm.

Here go left down the road past a white house and over a bridge to the outskirts of Alcester at Cold Comfort Lane. Cross the road and walk down Seggs Lane past a group of black and white cottages to the roundabout. Continue straight on till High Street meets the road, and turn right up it to return to the car park.

Coughton Court

Coughton Court, partly timber-framed, partly stone and brick ranged around three sides of a courtyard, has an instant romantic appeal. It was begun by Sir Robert Throckmorton at the opening of the reign of Henry VIII, and Sir Robert's son, Sir George Throckmorton, later 'built that stately castle-like gatehouse of free stone, intending (as it should seem), to have made the rest of his house suitable thereto'. (William Dugdale − Antiquities of Warwickshire p.751.)

The house replaced an earlier one, for the Throckmortons of Throckmorton in Worcestershire had been at Coughton since the early 15th century. They were ardent supporters of the Roman Communion and as a result suffered for their recusancy throughout much of the late Tudor and early Stuart period. In 1583 Nicholas Throckmorton was executed for his part in the Throckmorton Plot which aimed to depose Queen Elizabeth for Mary Queen of Scots. Mary Arden, the daughter of Sir Robert Throckmorton appears in a list of Warwickshire recusants in 1593, and owing to the suspicious character of those frequenting Coughton Court, in 1593 the Privy Council ordered her arrest.

During the Gunpowder Plot in 1605 many of the conspirators

97

were closely connected with the Throckmortons, and although Thomas Throckmorton went abroad, probably to avoid direct connection with the conspiracy, he lent his house to Sir Everard Digby, so that the Court became a headquarters, and later a refuge for the plotters at that critical time. Swift horses were kept ready in the stables, the Jesuit fathers Garrett and Greenway came to give mass to the conspirators' wives and Fathers Garrett and Tesimond appear to have been present when news of the plot's failure was brought. It is said that a room in the tower whose windows gave a wide view of the surrounding countryside was used as a chapel, whilst the priest, the sacred vessels and ornaments could be quickly concealed in a 'hide' below.

During the Civil War the Throckmortons took sides with the King, and when Parliamentary forces occupied the house in October 1643, a Royalist force set out from Worcester to relieve it, but turned back without making any attempt to engage the enemy garrison. In June 1644 at the approach of a large Royalist force the Parliamentarians withdrew, having first fired the house in three places.

That damage restored, Coughton Court was to suffer once more as a result of the Throckmortons' religious faith. In the reign of Charles II Sir Robert Throckmorton built a private chapel on the east side of the quadrangle and following the flight of James II on the 3rd December 1688, a day which was to become known locally as 'Running Thursday', a Protestant mob from Alcester sacked the interior of the chapel. The east wing was not entirely demolished as stated in the guide book, since an estate map of 1746 in the house shows the quadrangle as completely enclosed.

In 1780 another Sir Robert extended the wings on the west front and in 1795 his successor Sir John Throckmorton filled in the moat.

In 1945 the house was transferred to the National Trust and a careful restoration of the interior was carried out in 1956. Coughton Court is open to the public from Wednesday to Sunday, May to September in the afternoons, 2–5 pm, except Monday and Friday. Also in April and October on Saturdays and Sundays in the afternoons, and from Easter Monday to Thursday of Easter Week.

It is certainly worth a visit. The magnificent Tudor gatehouse, the centre piece of the facade, has above its wide entrance archway a two-storied oriel window flanked by smaller but still imposing side lights giving extensive views of the surroundings and surmounted by battlemented side towers. Thus the interior is well lit and it was in the first-floor drawing room that Lady Digby and her companions received the news of the failure of the Gunpowder Plot from Robert Catesby's servant Thomas Bates. A reminder of this event – so injurious to Catholics – is provided by the coats of arms of the families with whom the Throckmortons had shared so many dangers, on the panes of the window of the left-hand turret. The Throckmortons though, however closely linked with the Treshams and the Catesbys, were not a parochial family, and over the years had formed marriage alliances with other Catholics in Berkshire and Devon as well as Worcestershire and Warwickshire, and consequently had acquired estates in all these counties.

The gatehouse of course was originally approached by a drawbridge over the moat and though now only reminiscent of the days when such defences were essential, it has survived many hazards in its time. Elegant fan vaulting adorns the walls and ceiling of the ground floor, now known as the front hall, and the place no longer resounds to the clatter of hooves and the grinding of wheels.

The house is celebrated for its collection of family portraits, miniatures, tapestries, silver table ware and porcelain, and also for its hiding holes which were certainly made use of. Among other relics is the chemise worn by Mary Queen of Scots at her execution, and the 'Throckmorton Coat', made for a wager in a single day of 1811. Wool on two sheeps' backs at sunrise, it was a coat on a Throckmorton back at sunset. Both chemise and coat are in the saloon, which after the sacking of the chapel in the east wing was used for religious worship when allowed, until the Catholic church was built in 1855. Generations of Throckmortons lie buried and commemorated in the nearby parish church of St. Peter.

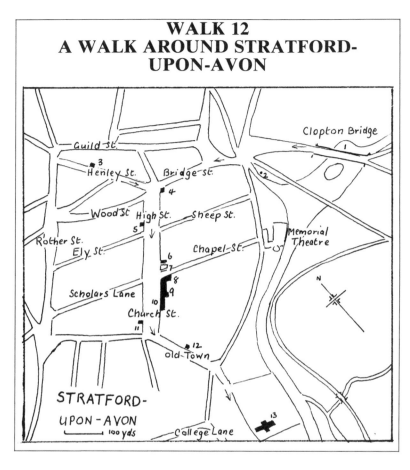

WALK 12
A WALK AROUND STRATFORD-UPON-AVON

Despite some intrusion of the Shakespeare interest, Stratford remains to-day a prosperous, attractive, bustling market town which also possesses a number of buildings of historical and architectural merit.

Fortunately Stratford escaped the Baedeker raids and most of the town which was known to Shakespeare has survived. Indeed the earliest ground plan shows three streets running parallel to the river and three crossing them at right angles which is largely the plan of the town centre to-day.

Follow Antonio's advice:

'beguile the time, and feed your knowledge
with viewing the town'.

(Twelfth Night Act III Scene iii).

1. Clopton Bridge. In the 15th century Hugh Clopton provided Stratford with 'a sumptuous new bridge and large of stone'. The wooden structure which it replaced had no causeway approach and was often dangerous to cross. John Leland writing in 1540 comments 'The bridge there was very smalle and ille, and at high waters very harde to passe by'.

Hugh Clopton was a native of Stratford who prospered as a merchant in London and became Mayor of that city in 1491. He returned to Stratford where he had built himself a fine town house, New Place in Chapel Street. He also had a house north of the town, Clopton House, which in 1605 was occupied by Ambrose Rokewood, one of the Gunpowder Plot conspirators. (See Walk 14)

2. Shakespeare Monument. Across this elegant bridge of 14 main arches, which to-day is a traffic bottleneck, are the Bancroft Gardens and the Shakespeare Monument unveiled in 1888, with a statue of the dramatist by Lord Ronald Sutherland Gower. The figures around the base – Hamlet, Prince Hal, Lady Macbeth and Falstaff – symbolise philosophy, history, tragedy and comedy.

Shakespeare's birthplace

3. The Birthplace. Probably the most visited literary shrine in England, this house in Henley Street is a neat timber-framed

101

structure dating from the early 16th century. John Shakespeare had a business here as a fell-monger and glove-maker and in the living quarters William Shakespeare was born on the 23 April 1564.

In 1601 the house and business premises were inherited by Shakespeare who bequeathed them in his will to his sister Joan Hart. On her death in 1664 the property went to Shakespeare's eldest daughter Susannah Hall and it remained in the family until 1806 when it was sold and converted, one part into a butcher's shop and the other into an inn called the 'Maidenhead'.

In 1847 the two premises were bought by public subscription as a national memorial to be vested in the Shakespeare Birthday Trust, and restored as far as possible to their original state. To-day the Trust owns also the New Place Estate, Nash's house, Hall's Croft, Anne Hathaway's cottage at Shottery and Mary Arden's house at Wilmcote.

The Birthplace still retains some of its original timbers and stonework. Several of the fireplaces are original and the whole building has been furnished in the contemporary style. The entrance opens into what was the living room, with a kitchen at the back. The oak staircase leads to the front bedroom which, it is presumed, was the birth room and where window panes and walls have since been defaced with the scratchings and scribblings of numerous vandals of past generations – some of them quite noteworthy, – Isaac Walton, Thomas Carlyle, Sir Walter Scott, Sir Henry Irving, Helen Terry.

The other rooms are largely filled with exhibition items – documents relation to the poet and his family, portraits of the dramatist, and Elizabethan books.

On the ground floor the living room is connected with what was the workroom and shop, and is now a museum showing the history and associations of the house. The present order and dignity did not always prevail here. The Jubilee celebrations at Stratford in September 1769 were to bring a steadily increasing influx of Shakespeare pilgrims to the Birthplace, where the Harts had assembled a ludicrous collection of Shakespeare 'relics' to charm and amaze the credulous. 'Shakespeare's old chair' was cut up and sold many times over!

In 1795 half of the Birthplace building was leased to Thomas Hornby, a butcher, whose wife claimed descent from Shakespeare, and the pair set up a most profitable business selling 'Shakespeare relics', which included two chairs allegedly given to the poet by the

Earl of Southampton, an old sword which, it was said, Shakespeare had used when playing Hamlet, a painting of Shakespeare as Petruchio painted by his nephew William Shakespeare, and the gun which was used in the famous poaching incident at Charlecote Park!

By now the Birth-room walls were covered with 'signatures' of visitors, amongst them many celebrated and titled personalities from all over Europe, which the curious were eager to pay extra to see. Mary Hornby was not content with this largesse however. Apparently some of Shakespeare's genius had been passed down, for Mary in a fit of poetic frenzy composed a tragedy, 'the most execrable verses that folly ever produced, 'wrote one critic. Yet the credulous were impressed. Even the Prince Regent professed interest and sought to buy 'Shakespeare's sword'.

The landlord of the property was equally impressed with the ever growing flood of pilgrims to the shrine in Henley Street. He doubled and redoubled the rent and in 1820 Mary Hornby now a widow, was compelled to move across the street and take with her the precious 'relics', but not before she had whitewashed the walls of the Birth-room and obliterated the famous 'signatures'. 'At one fell swoop, out went the illustrious signatures of kings, queens, princes, princesses, ambassadors, bishops, Lord Chancellors, Lord Chief Justices Etc.' Mrs Court, the new tenant of the Birthplace quickly remedied this piece of spiteful vandalism. The walls of the Birth-room were whitewashed afresh and the 'signatures' were there once more for all to gape at. Now the eager pilgrims had the added attraction of the rival purveyors of Shakespeare wonders abusing each other across the street.

When Mrs Court died in 1846 the property was up for auction and rumours circulated that Phineas T. Barnum the showman wanted to buy it to transfer it across the Atlantic. The Shakespeare Birthday Committee was hurriedly formed and money was raised to buy the proporty. Most of the adjoining buildings were pulled down, – the barns, brewhouse, piggeries and outhouses which had long surrounded it finally disappeared.

4. Judith Quiney's House. At the corner of High Street and facing a frantic traffic island is a superb timber-framed dwelling which was once the home of Shakespeare's daughter Judith who married a vintner, Thomas Quiney.

To-day it houses an extremely busy Information Bureau. Beneath it is a fine stone-vaulted crypt. The building was at one time used as a jail and was known as the 'Cage'.

5. *Harvard House.* On the west side of the High Street and next door to the Garrick Inn, the splendid timber-framed building with the richly carved front is Harvard house.

Built in 1596 by a properous Stratford butcher, alderman and bailiff, Thomas Rogers, whose initials appear on the front with those of his wife Anne, the house is an excellent example of a late Elizabethan town house. During his term of office Rogers was accused by the Council of forestalling the grain market, to which he replied, 'I care not a turd for them all'.

He certainly prospered and when his house in High Street was destroyed by fire in 1595 he rebuilt in a most ornate style. Much of the ground floor frontage is original, and almost every timber is richly carved. The breast-summers or exterior beams are all beautifully treated with fleur-de-lis in high relief. Bracket-heads carry the bear and ragged staffs of the Warwick Earls and a bull's head over a mutilated female head.

On the top floor a row of corbels all have finely carved human faces. Inside, on the ground floor there is an exceptionally fine raftered ceiling and some excellent oak panelling.

Thomas Rogers' daughter Katherine married Robert Harvard, a prosperous butcher of Southwark, and John Harvard the son of that marriage was educated at Emmanuel College, Cambridge, emigrated to the North American colonies in 1637, and founded Harvard University at Cambridge, Massachusetts.

Much restored in the early 20th century under the direction of the novelist Marie Corelli, Rogers' house was bought by a wealthy Chicago benefactor Edward Morris in 1909, and presented to Harvard University.

6. *Nash's House.* In Chapel Street is another well-preserved timber-framed house which once belonged to Thomas Nash, the first husband of Shakespeare's grand-daughter Elizabeth Hall who later became Lady Barnard. This house which was extensively restored early in the present century contains 16th and 17th century furniture as well as the ancient muniment chest which was originally the property of the Guild of the Holy Cross.

The upper storey now provides an interesting local museum displaying some pre-historic remains, a little Roman pottery, some finds from the Anglo-Saxon burial ground discovered at Alveston and a number of documents relating to Stratford.

7. *New Place.* At the corner of Chapel Street and Chapel Lane is the site of New Place, Leland's 'praty howse of brike and tymber',

which was built by Hugh Clopton around 1483, and which William Shakespeare bought in 1596 for £60.

The house which was 'in great ryne and decay' was restored by Shakespeare who lived there from 1610 until his death in April 1616. It was bequeathed to his daughter Susannah Hall and after her death to her daughter Lady Barnard. Later it was sold to the beneficiaries of the will of Lady Barnard and eventually reverted to the Clopton family.

In 1702 Sir John Clopton decided to replace the house with one in a more modern style and the greater part of Shakespeare's New Place was pulled down. In 1753 the house Clopton built was bought by the Vicar, the Reverend Francis Gastrell, a canon of Lichfield cathedral.

Gastrell, a rather irascible individual, deeply resented the curiosity of visitors who wished to see inside the house and sit under the famous mulberry tree which Shakespeare was said to have planted in the garden. In 1756, maintaining that the tree overshadowed his windows and made the house damp, he had it cut down, much to the fury of the people of Stratford who registered their disapproval by stoning the reverend's windows.

Thomas Sharp who mended clocks for a living, recognised the opportunity offered by the disaster, bought the mulberry logs and began the unlimited production of drinking cups, bowls and boxes made from the Shakespeare mulberry tree. Indeed a whole grove of mulberry trees could not have provided the Shakespeare mulberry drinking cups etc. which were to leave Stratford in the next generation.

In the meantime the Reverend Gastrell was having endless trouble with Stratford Corporation. He objected to the rates which he had to pay for New Place and its dilapidated barns. In 1758 he demolished three of the barns but the Corporation insisted that he should pay the full rate. In 1759 Gastrell had the whole building razed to the ground 'amidst the rage and curses of the inhabitants' of Stratford. The site was bought by the Trust and laid out as an attractive garden to enclose the foundations.

8. Guild Chapel. The Guild Chapel on the corner of Chapel Lane and Church Street was founded in 1296 by Robert de Stratford as a chapel for the Guild of the Holy Cross. John de Stratford at one time Rector of Holy Trinity became Archbishop of Canterbury, Lord Chancellor and an adviser of the young King Edward III.

The chancel was rebuilt in 1450 and the nave in 1490. Above the *chancel arch is an early 16th century Doom or Day of Judgement.*

The Guild of the Holy Cross was dissolved in 1547 and in 1553 the Crown granted the chapel to Stratford Corporation. To-day it is used by King Edward's School next door.

9. Guild Hall. Adjoining the chapel in Church Street is the Guild Hall, another fine timber-framed building which was originally the headquarters of the Guild of the Holy Cross.

Since 1553 the upper hall has been used by King Edward's Grammar School and there has been a school on this site since 1401. The adjacent pedagogue's House was built by the Guild in 1426 to accommodate the Master of the School.

10. Almshouses. Next to the Guildhall is a long row of well-preserved almshouses built by the Guild of the Holy Cross in the 15th century and still providing pleasant, cosy homes for 22 aged people of the town.

11. Mason Croft. On the opposite side of Church Street is Mason Croft, a neat, attractive brick-built house of the middle of the 18th century which was once the home of Marie Corelli, who died here in 1924. Marie Corelli appeared in Stratford in 1899 and accompanied by her Belgian companion, Bertha Vyver, moved into Hall's Croft. She had established some fame as a writer of best-selling romantic novels of which 'Barabas' (1893), and 'The Sorrows of Satan' (1895) were probably the best known. The style is so pretentious, sentimental, melodramatic, and overlaid with such arrant pseudo-philosophical moral preaching, as to make the novels quite unreadable today. Yet as a novelist Marie Corelli had thousands of devoted readers and admirers, including Meredith, Gladstone, Tennyson, Oscar Wilde and Edward VII, who invited her to his coronation. Queen Victoria was of the opinion that the novels of Marie Corelli would long outlive those of George Eliot! When Marie died in 1924 'Barabas' was in its 54th edition and 'the Sorrows of Satan' in its 60th!

Miss Corelli was clearly bent on establishing social ascendancy in Stratford as the chief interpreter and doyenne of the Shakespeare Cult. In 1901 she took over Mason Croft and immediately set about refurbishing it in such a vulgar, idiosyncratic manner as to verge on vandalism. She attracted fair attention which she encouraged by her extravagant, flamboyant dress, and her affected, ostentatious manner. At the celebration of Shakespeare's birthday she produced an enormous wreath of flowers which she claimed had been gathered in Dante's garden in Florence.

When Sarah Bernhardt arrived in Stratford to join Frank Benson's Company, Marie met her at the station 'attired in cream lisse, trimmed with Venetian guipure lace, and wore a gold and white toque trimmed with black tips and osprey.' With her equally stout, dumpy companion she was carried around the town in a tiny chaise drawn by a pair of Shetland ponies named Puck and Ariel. Later she imported a Venetian gondola complete with Italian gondolier in costume, and the quaint pair were poled up and down the Avon. Unfortunately the gondolier pined for Venice and found solace in the ale served in the 'Dirty Duck'. As a result he was often unfit to steer his craft on the busy river, and eventually he had to be replaced by a local, more temperate oarsman.

When she died, Marie Corelli had long been a forgotten figure in Stratford. Her companion lived on in Mason Croft until 1939. In her will Marie wished Mason Croft to be preserved as a shrine for artists, scientists and distinguished foreigners, but on the death of Miss Vyver the will was declared invalid and the property was sold. Today it serves the postgraduate English School of Birmingham University.
12. Hall's Croft. Turning left from Church Street into the Old Town, discover another charming timber-framed dwelling which was once the home of Susannah Shakespeare and her husband Dr. John Hall from 1607–1616 when the couple moved to New Place.

The lower storey has a frame of vertical oak timbers standing on a stone ground-sill with the intervals between the timbers filled with lath and plaster. The overhanging upper storey rests on brackets carved from the upright posts and the gabled, tiled roof is surmounted by clusters of picturesque chimney stacks.

A sturdy 17th century staircase leads to the upper rooms where the main item of interest is a splendidly carved Tudor bedstead with crisp linenfold panelling at the head.

At the rear of the house is the dispensary and pharmacy used by Dr. Hall who was quite a well-known physician.
13. Holy Trinity Church. An avenue of lime trees leads to Holy Trinity Church which has a most idyllic site on the west bank of the River Avon.

The nave and transepts are largely 14th century, the chancel with its splendid perpendicular window is late 15th century.

The chancel is entered through an early 16th century screen and on the north wall of the sanctuary is the monument to William Shakespeare with the earliest authenticated statue of the dramatist made by Gerard Jansen about 1623.

Unfortunately in 1861 it was decided that the bust looked rather drab and it was 'beautified', which meant coating it with rather garish colours.

Shakespeare's grave is in the floor beneath the monument and to the left is the grave of his wife Anne Hathaway who died in 1623. To the right are the graves of Shakespeare's eldest daughter Susannah (died 1649), her husband Dr. John Hall (died 1635) and Thomas Nash (died 1647), the first husband of Shakespeare's granddaughter Elizabeth Hall.

Shakespearean Properties open to the public:

		November – March	April – October
The Birthplace	Weekdays	9 am – 4.30pm	9am – 6pm
	Sundays	1.30pm – 4.30pm	10am – 6pm
Hall's Croft			
New Place	Weekdays	9am – 4.30pm	9 am – 6pm
Nash's House	Sundays	Not open	10am – 6pm

WALK 13
STRATFORD − LUDDINGTON −
SHOTTERY − STRATFORD.

O. S. Sheet No. 151 1:50,000 Stratford-upon-Avon.
Distance 7 miles approx. Start point and car park
College Lane. Grid Ref. 20,544.

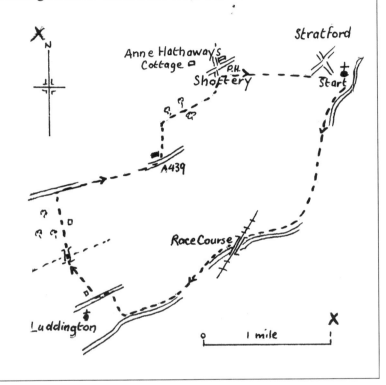

The going can be muddy in winter, and a ploughed field is almost
inevitable nowadays, but the route is always clear and the river
banks are usually interesting with flowers and glimpses of water
fowl. Shottery is a village with its own history and for the confirmed
walker is a good point to aim for.

Energy left after the town tour can be put to good use by starting
the walk from College Lane and going down Mill Lane to the right

of the church, passing on the right the garden of Avon Field and then the former nunnery, Soli House. On the left are the new flats which were erected on the site of Lucy's Mill, and the river path begins by passing under a bridge to the first meadow alongside the Avon. It continues past a weir and eyot with a lock and bridge, crosses a stile and arrives at a footbridge into the next meadow which is flanked by a spinney. Then comes a bridge under the railway, constructed in solid brickwork and having an interesting vista of the receding piers of the short viaduct. Stratford Racecourse is on the right, and the way goes to the left to rejoin the river bank. The buildings of Luddington are now in sight over the next field and after following the bend in the stream the path comes to a footbridge at the backs of some houses.

Now it is necessary to follow the line of the path as it passes behind the houses, climbing a short wooden staircase and descending again to a wire fence, and winding along the river bank which has in places been almost incorporated into the gardens of the residences. It passes through gates, alongside boats and through lawns, but nowhere is it blocked, and eventually it emerges into open country again and traverses a long field much favoured by mallards and Canada geese. Pollarded willows line the opposite bank. There are two more stiles in wooden fences and then a green arrow on a white background suggests a diversion right uphill at a stand of poplars. Two stiles admit to a pasture which must be crossed half left to a metal gate and finger post at the top of the slope.

Turn left along the road past Boddington Farm and the houses until the small village green is reached. Here go right, in front of a rather splendid thatched house. Luddington is a straggling community, but clearly this was the village centre in former days. Pass over a white stile to the left of a bungalow with a green chain-link fence, and then through a metal gate into an orchard. Go uphill past a pond on the left to a fence and stile in the corner and then follow the tall hedge on the left of the next field over a disused railway bridge which is a good vantage point for views of Stratford to the right. Continue on the same heading straight ahead keeping the hedge on the right over two more fields, gradually descending towards a group of farm buildings. On the right the caravan site at Dodwell Park is visible. Pass through a patch of rough scrub and a gate alongside the buildings to emerge on to the A439 Stratford — Evesham road. Turn right up it.

There is a pavement, fortunately, for now comes a tedious stretch of about a mile alongside this busy road. On the right is the main entrance to the caravan site, on the left a farm road which has a pair of Napoleonic cannon for gateposts. Keep going to the top of Bordon Hill where there are good views. At a car sale site on the left go down the path just in front of the red letter box to a facing gate. The path actually passes along the right-hand boundary of the site. Through the gate a muddy track begins, going down through hedges till it swings right and becomes grassy for a while. Follow it left, then right, by the side of a wood until it reaches Shottery, passing in front of a bungalow and coming out on to the road at a school. Turn left and admire one of the few timber-framed schools in the district – Shottery St. Andrew National School, 1870. It carries initials and an anchor in the brick infill. Turn left and the welcoming 'Bell' faces you.

After refreshment, return to the start by taking the road facing the 'Bell' and going past the Post Office on the right to the black and white houses at Tavern Lane. Turn right, then left along the Public Footpath which passes between schools on the left and right, then crosses a common and heads straight for the church spire. It goes over the road at a housing estate and across the old railway, then the Evesham road. Keep going straight on down Chestnut Walk to Old Town, leaving Hall's Croft on the left and arriving soon at the church and College Lane.

Anne Hathaway's Cottage.
The cottage is little over a mile from Stratford, and is just beyond the crossroads, and to the right, as Celia directs Oliver:

> *'West of this place, down in the neighbourhood bottom;*
> *The rank of osiers, by the neighbourhood stream,*
> *Left on your right hand, brings you to the place.'*
> > *(As You Like It Act IV, sc.iii.)*

The cottage was the 12 roomed farmhouse of a successful yeoman farmer, a fine timber-framed building with a thatched roof. It was built in the 15th century on a slope and therefore arranged on several levels. Severely damaged by fire in 1969 it has been restored with the utmost care.

The house was the home of Anne Hathaway from her birth in 1556 to her marriage with Shakespeare in 1582, and it remained the property of the Hathaway family until it was acquired by the Shakespeare Birthday Trust in 1982. The interior has some 16th

111

century fireplaces and a fair collection of domestic utensils and old furniture, including the 'courting settle' said to have been used by Shakespeare and Anne, and the famous 'second best bed' left by Shakespeare to his wife in his will.

Anne Hathaway's Cottage is open to the public:

	November – March	April – October
Weekdays	9 am – 4.30pm	9 am – 6pm
Sundays	1.30pm – 4.30pm	10am – 6pm

WALK 14
WELCOMBE ROAD — WELCOMBE HILL
— ROUND HOUSE FARM —
WELCOMBE ROAD.

O.S. Sheet No. 151 1:50,000 Stratford-upon-Avon.
Distance 4 miles. Start point and car park, Welcombe
Road, Grid Ref. 205552.

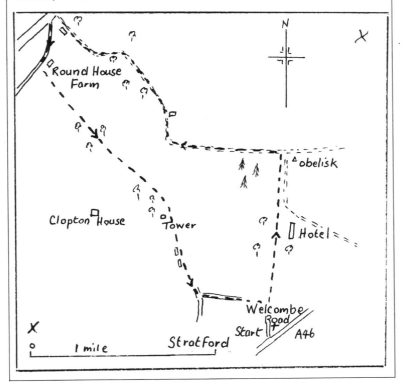

This is a popular local walk, largely over springy turf or along good
farm tracks and offering splendid views over the countryside.

Walk up Welcombe Road and at the bend at the top, go through
a kissing gate to take the footpath signposted to Ingon. Follow the
path across the pasture with a tall hedge on the right and the folly of
Clopton Tower in view on the slope to the left ahead. Through a

113

kissing gate swing slightly left to go over the brow of the slope and come upon yet another kissing gate.

Walk on across pleasantly landscaped country-side to pass the Welcombe Hotel on the right. Several paths lie ahead which all meander through the dingle to converge at another metal kissing gate in the fence on the hillside. Through the gate turn right to examine the tall, striking obelisk which is a well-known landmark in the area. The hillock which has traces of ridge and furrow, gives a commanding view east across to the wooded slopes of Edge Hill.

From the obelisk return to the track and follow the path which goes through a metal gate and leads past a noble stand of pines on the left. Pass the trees to go through another metal gate and enter a good farm track which runs for some distance between hedgerows, swings right then left past the farm, and then winds around a wood on the left. At the end of the wood the track turns right once more and climbs past another farm on the left to emerge on the road — now a busy bypass. Turn left away from the bypass along the old road which goes downhill to reach an unusual, castellated Round House Farm, on the left.

Just beyond the farm entrance find a signposted footpath which runs between a wire fence on the right and a tall hedge on the left. We now have delightful views on the right across the Arden Valley to the distant Malvern Hills. Keep on the same heading through a hunting gate, over metal railings and then along an enclosed, and sometimes rather overgrown footpath which skirts the edge of a straggling spinney. In wet weather this part of the ramble can be rather muddy. Fortunately it is just for a few hundred yards. Through a hunting gate emerge near the stand of pines now on the left.

Go right and follow the path which runs alongside the wire fence on the right. The path widens and descends through a wood which was probably planted to shelter game birds, and which today is a favourite haunt of green woodpeckers. With luck you may hear their curious, intriguing bursts of staccato tappings or their ludicrous, laughing call. Keep on the same heading to come upon the Clopton Tower built to add romantic interest to the prospect of Clopton House away to the right. Climb a stile to the left of the Tower and follow the well-marked path down the slope to reach a kissing gate which gives onto an enclosed path at the bottom of a row of gardens. The path opens onto Maidenhead Road. Keep on the same heading to turn left along Benton Road and so into Welcombe Road.

1. Welcombe Hotel. There are records of a manor on the site in the 13th century, and in Shakespeare's day the house and estate was owned by William Combe the High Sheriff who was reputed to be the richest man in the area. His wealth it seems had come from his uncle John Combe who lent money at interest. In 1614 William Combe was to cause a great stir locally when he attempted to enclose the Welcombe Lands for sheep farming by employing men to make ditches and dig out the ridges of tilling. His tenants petitioned the Assize Court at Warwick and the presiding judge, Sir Edward Coke, ordered that Combe 'should never enclose nor lay downe his common arable land.' Combe persisted however and was only stopped in 1619 when he was ordered by the Privy Council to restore the land he had enclosed, and abide by the ruling of the Court of Assize. He finally capitulated, and on the payment of a fine of four pounds, was granted 'his pardon for enclosing.'

In the 17th century the house passed to John Lloyd of Snitterfield, and in 1842 it was bought by Mark Philip, a successful cotton manufacturer from Manchester, who largely built the present house. He was succeeded by his brother Robert Philip and then Robert's son-in-law, Sir George Trevelyan, who was President of the Board of Trade in Gladstone's third government. His son, the historian G.M. Trevelyan, was born at Welcombe in 1876. In 1931 the house was bought by the London, Midland and Scottish Railway Company and before World War II the Welcombe Hotel was one of that company's best known hotels. Today it is a popular hotel especially with golfers.

2 The Welcombe Hill obelisk. This striking, graceful monument which is 120 feet high and made of Welsh granite, was erected in 1876 by Robert Philip at a cost of £4,000 to commemorate his brother Mark Philip. On the west side of the monument the inscription relates that Mark Philip was born at Park Prestwich, Lancashire on the 4th November, 1800 and died at Welcombe, Stratford-upon-Avon on the 23rd December, 1873. On the passing of the Reform Bill in 1832 he was elected the first member of parliament for Manchester, which he represented for fifteen years. He was also active in the cause of education, civil and religious liberties and commercial freedom. The east side of the monument bears the Philip coat of arms in strong, crisp relief.

Welcombe Hill was the scene of a very brief skirmish during the Civil War. In January 1643 Stratford was occupied by a troop of royalist horse commanded by Colonel Wagstaffe. Early on the morning of the 25th February Lord Brooke led a parliamentary force out of Warwick, hoping to surprise the royalists but 'a countryman and friend of theirs espying us two miles on this side, crossed the fields and gave the enemy advertisement: upon which they drew themselves out under a hill, where they could view us in our march.' Lord Brooke was a seasoned campaigner. He brought up his artillery and took up his position on the slope north of Welcombe Hill near Ingon.

The royalists were thrown into utter confusion by the first salvo. 'From the reer division we let flie a drake which ran through the midst of them and forced them to wheele off towards the Town and we hastened after them so fast as our Carriages and the Plow'd land so well softened with the raine would permit us.' (Last weeks Proceedings of the Lord Brooke, and the first in His Present Expedition — March 1643). A drake or sake was a light field piece which fired a 5lb shot, and had a maximum range of 1500 yards.

Learning that the parliamentarians planned to hold a military council in the town hall, which was also used as an ammunition store, and no doubt hoping to redeem his reputation after his sorry showing at Welcombe Hill, Colonel Wagstaffe came stealthily into the town at night. Under the town hall he laid a train of gunpowder with a slow match, which he believed he had timed to explode when the enemy council was sitting. Unfortunately he had mistimed the fuse and the explosion was premature. The parliamentarians were unharmed and the town hall, which was less than ten tears old, was completely demolished!

3. Clopton House. The house dates from the 16th century and was much enlarged in the 17th century by Sir John Clopton. It was re-modelled again in the early 18th century and today only the east front has retained the original timber frame, the rest of the house is in brick.

Two of the Clopton family were singularly unfortunate in Shakespeare's day. Charlotte Clopton was accidentally buried alive in the family vault during the plague outbreak that ravaged Stratford in 1564, and the dreadful incident probably gave the dramatist the idea for the vault scene in Romeo and Juliet. (Romeo and Juliet — Act V, sc. iii). About twenty years later Margaret Clopton, disappointed in love, drowned herself in a pond behind the house and it is suggested gave Shakespeare the inspiration for Ophelia's watery death in Hamlet. (Hamlet — Act IV, sc. vii).

In the reign of Elizabeth I William Clopton was fined as a Popish recusant and in the roof of the house is an attic bed-chamber where the walls are decorated with texts and where presumably mass was said during those penal times.

In 1605 Ambrose Rokewood, one of the Gunpowder Conspirators rented the house from Lord Carew, and when the plot failed, the bailiff of Stratford, supported by the local militia descended upon the house and seized there a bag 'containing copes, vestments, crosses, crucifixes, chalices, and other massing relics.'

WALK 15
HAMPTON LUCY – DAISY HILL FARM
– MOUNT PLEASANT FARM
– HAMPTON LUCY.

O.S. Sheet No. 151 1:50,000 Stratford-upon-Avon.
Distance 3½ miles. Start point and car park, lane
outside Hampton Lucy Church. Grid Ref. 571257.

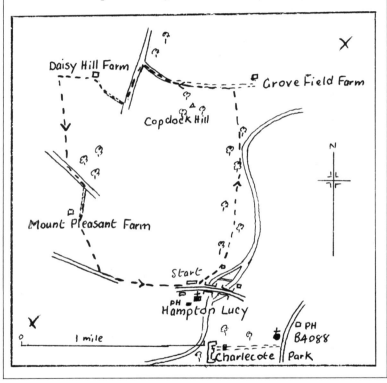

Two villages, each of differing and individual character, a mellow
country house set in a dream-like park, two churches as dissimilar as
the villages they serve, and a restored working mill form the
interesting background for this walk. The route begins by crossing
a ridge giving good views over the Avon and the hamlet of
Wasperton, then covers several fields, some of them arable, and

118

lanes before completing the circle and returning through Hampton Lucy to the start point. It can be muddy and is undulating in parts, but its interest is enhanced by the literary and historical associations with an area for so long the domain of one of Warwickshire's most famous families, the Lucys of Charlecote.

From Hampton Lucy church turn right and walk to the single span iron bridge over the Avon. The bridge, cast at the Horseley works in Shropshire in 1829, was the gift of the Rector of Hampton Lucy, the Rev. John Lucy, who also contributed to the rebuilding of the great church in 1826.

Go down a vehicle track on the left by the river and after 100 yards climb a stile into a paddock at the corner of a spinney. Follow the path along the edge of the spinney to go through a gate and where the way divides, take the upper path through the trees. Through another gate the path skirts the edge of an arable field with the wood on the right. Go through a second waymarked gate and then emerge on rough open ground from which there are good views of the river and of the Warwickshire countryside as far as the elegant tower of St. Mary's church at Warwick in the distance ahead.

Through a gate the path goes along the edge of an arable field where the farmer has left a good headland. In the distance to the left can be seen the slender obelisk on Welcombe Hill east of Stratford which was erected in 1876 in memory of Mark Philip who was Manchester's first M.P. (1832–47) (see Walk 14)

Continue with the hedge on the right to go past an old water tank and walk through a gap where the gate is broken, to continue on the same heading across an arable field past four oaks in line, all that remains of an ancient hedgerow. The path dips to a tall hedge at the bottom of Copdock Hill. Turn right, and keeping the hedge on the left drop down to the left-hand corner of the field. Go left through a gap and walk along another arable field with the hedge again on the left, to cross a stream and reach a metalled track leading to Grove Field Farm.

Turn left to reach a road and go left again, and after ⅓ mile near the top of the slope, go along the track on the right which leads to Daisy Hill Farm. Follow the track to the farm, go left through the farm yard at the rear of the house and come to a metal gate. Descend a sheep pasture to cross a rather difficult triple stile. Climb along the edge of an arable field with the hedgerow on the left. After ⅓ mile the hedge turns sharp left, turn left and follow the line of the hedge around a large arable field to reach the road leading to Hampton Lucy.

Turn left on the road and after ½ mile go down the track which leads to Mount Pleasant Farm on the right. Keep left of the farm buildings which are boldly marked A.D. 1806, and join the path which runs by the hedge on the left. Follow the line of the hedge for a considerable way to reach an incomplete step stile in the left-hand corner of the field. Over the stile strike straight across the arable field to reach a wide metal gate giving on to the road. Turn left and walk into Hampton Lucy and refreshment at the 'Boar's Head', or if preferred at the 'Charlecote Pheasant' about ½ mile further on.

Charlecote and the Lucys.

As the Avon winds its gentle way through the meadows it passes through Charlecote Park and flows below the walls of the Elizabethan-style home of the Lucys who have lived here since the 12th century.

The park has an abundance of fine trees, including the magnificent avenue of limes seen from the west lodge, though the great elms once lining the way to the Gatehouse have long since succumbed to Dutch Elm disease and been replaced by Turkey oaks. It is stocked with fallow and red deer, and a herd of Jacob sheep introduced 200 years ago. The deer are often to be seen grazing near the little Gothic revival church by the roadside. In 1769 the park was improved by Capability Brown, commissioned by George Lucy in the sum of £525 to 'alter the slopes and give a natural level corresponding with the house on every side'. The result of his work is the gracious enclosure we see today, fenced round by oak paling said to date from Elizabethan times, and watered by the Avon and its tributary the little Hele which joins it behind the house.

Part of the Charlecote folk-lore is the story that William Shakespeare, caught poaching a deer in the park, was brought before the first Sir Thomas in the house and summarily punished, possibly by fining and flogging, whereupon he removed to London and later caricatured Sir Thomas as Justice Shallow in Henry IV pt. II and the Merry Wives. The incident and its sequel may have some truth in it, for the poet makes a point of referring to the 'dozen white Luces' in the Justice's old coat while Shallow himself taxes Falstaff with killing his deer, beating his men and breaking fences. (Merry Wives of Windsor – Act 1, sc.i.). Later Shakespeare, now respectable and responsible, returned to Stratford and as far as is known, lived on good terms with the Lucys thereafter.

'Cherlecote' came into the possession of Sir Walter de Cherlecote in 1189 and his grandson Sir William adopted the name 'de Lucy' because his wife was one of the de Lucy family of Cockermouth. There followed other Lucys, including Sir Edward, a Lancastrian soldier under Henry VII, until the first Sir Thomas came into the property in 1551. He it was who with his wife, the rich heiress Joyce Acton, rebuilt the present house and he was knighted here in 1565 by Robert Dudley, acting on behalf of Queen Elizabeth. In 1572 he entertained the Queen at Charlecote after she had been staying at Kenilworth as the guest of the same Robert, now Earl of Leicester, and in his capacity as magistrate probably punished Shakespeare.

Two more Sir Thomases followed, to be succeeded by Sir Richard, M.P. for Warwick and Sheriff in 1647. Jumping a century we come to George Lucy, who died in 1786. It was he who employed Capability Brown to redesign the parkland. He built the present bridge over the brook after he had diverted the Warwick-Stratford road away from the house. He died unmarried and was succeeded by his cousin the Reverend Hammond, whose son George Hammond Lucy married a Welsh heiress, Mary Elizabeth Williams. Together they built the wing containing the dining room and library.

Henry Spencer Lucy, the surviving second son of Mary Elizabeth, presided over the estate at a time of declining fortunes for land-owners and of real crisis for English agriculture. Through inability to let his farms at economic rents, his income was severely reduced, yet he continued to live in as lavish a manner as ever, enjoying his country pursuits, especially hunting and shooting. He was the last of the Lucys to enjoy his patrimony in the time-honoured way. His daughter Ada married in 1892 Sir Henry Ramsey-Fairfax and henceforth the family name became Fairfax-Lucy. Their son Sir Montgomery presented the property to the National Trust in 1945, and his descendants still occupy quarters in the house, though the chief glories of the place, the fine library and furniture, the portraits brought home by various members of the Lucy family from their continental tours, are in the care of the Trust.

Not the least interesting features of Charlecote are the Gatehouse, containing a collection of family sporting regalia, the Brew House and Kitchen, still intact and a good illustration of how independent and self-supporting the great country houses were in their hey-day. The stables and coach houses contain the family saddlery and carriages, including the Travelling Coach which was used for those months-long journeys on the Continent, following the Grand Tour which was considered essential to a gentleman's education.

The two churches in the vicinity are St. Leonard's on the edge of the park, and St. Peter's at Hampton Lucy. They are both products of the early Victorian religious revival when both faith and funds seemed unlimited. St. Leonard's, built in 1850 on the site of its small 12th century predecessor, was entirely paid for by Mary Elizabeth Lucy, the widow of George Lucy who died in 1845. The lady survived her husband by 45 years and devoted herself to her numerous family, most of whom predeceased her, and the house and estate. She was clearly a woman of much charm and wit, elegant and fashionable, moving easily in the aristocratic circles of the country. Her diaries, which are eminently readable, convey a good picture of the life of a country lady of the time, and appear under the title 'Mistress of Charlecote', introduced by Lady Fairfax-Lucy.

The church was conceived in the Victorian Gothic style by the architect John Gibson as a memorial to George Lucy, and contains the family chapel and the vault where Mary Elizabeth lies. In the chapel are the tombs of three Sir Thomas Lucys. On the right are the first Sir Thomas, possibly the model for Justice Shallow, and his wife Joyce, both effigies in alabaster. In the centre are the third Sir Thomas and his wife Alice, the effigies in black and white marble being most impressive and were long attributed to Bernini. This Sir Thomas was a man of two great passions — riding and learning, hence the representation on the monument of a horseman and the works of classical authors. The second Sir Thomas and his second wife Constance, with their many children, are on the left of the entry. Constance erected her husband's tomb, and on her death her effigy in mourning attire, and in a kneeling position, was added to it.

Those who find the Gothic Revival style rather pretentious and fussy will at least concede that St. Leonard's has the virtue of being small; not so its massive neighbour St. Peter's across the park at Hampton Lucy. Here the medieval church was completely demolished in 1826 and the present building was erected at the expense of the Rector, the Reverend John Lucy, as a pioneer church in the new style. As such, it must have considerable interest for the student of architecture, but as a parish church in a small village, it is overwhelming and ostentatious. Its architect Thomas Rickman had as his avowed aim 'to adapt the beautiful details and decorations of ancient work to modern purposes,' and his adaptation at Hampton Lucy is certainly thorough and complete. The east end, much the best feature, was remodelled in 1858 by Sir Gilbert Scott, and the windows there illuminate the otherwise gloomy interior, catching the eye immediately on entry.

The rectory south west of the church is a handsome late 17th century house of red brick with stone string courses, angle dressings and a moulded cornice and balusters. The house is generally accepted to be the work of Francis Smith of Warwick. (see Walk 1) Also just outside the village is a working mill grinding corn, which can be visited at weekends in the summer months.

Charlecote House and Park are open to the public May to the end of September, every day except Monday and Thursday from 11 am to 5 pm, and on Bank Holidays. Also on Saturdays and Sundays in April and October.

WALK 16
COMBROOK – COMPTON VERNEY
– COMBROOK.

O.S. Sheet No. 151 1:50,000 Stratford-upon-Avon. Distance 4 miles. Car park and start point, lane by Combrook Church. Grid Ref. 307519.

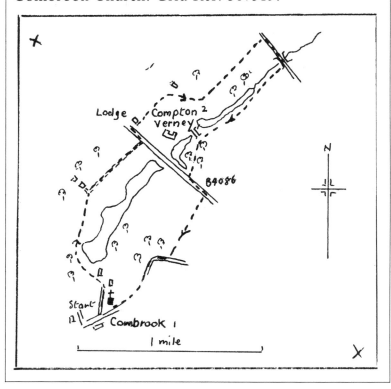

This is an idyllic ramble across well-kept park land and along firm farm tracks, with the superb backcloth of a fine Palladian country house seen across the lake. The going is firm and where there are crops, a good headland has been left for ramblers.

Park neatly in the lane by the church and walk along the no through road to go past a covered well and turn left into a signposted, narrow path just before a row of old cottages. The path goes down over a brook in the hollow, and then climbs to the right up a slope to a hunting gate. Carry on across a field to enter a wood, and skirt the edge of the lake to go through another hunting gate. This short track through the wood is rather cut up by horses, and could be muddy in wet weather. Now go straight ahead across a springy sheep pasture to reach a metal gate, then follow the bridle path which leads to a metalled drive serving the farm on the left. Turn right on the drive and continue across the parkland to reach the main road.

Turn left, walk up the hill and turn right along the drive which goes past Compton Verney Lodge. Follow this firm track which leads away from the Lodge, cross the intersection of tracks, and continue for a few hundred yards to turn right in front of a series of large barns, and go downhill though a wide gateway. Where the track forks go left. Compton Verney house is now clearly in view with the delightful Adam bridge at the bottom of the slope. Continue on the well-trodden track for about a mile to reach the road. Turn right and soon go over a small bridge. Over the bridge turn immediately right to walk along the headland on the right of the arable field and alongside the stream on the left.

Keep alongside the stream to reach the bridge designed by Robert Adam more than 200 years ago. We must emphasise that the bridge and the property across the bridge are strictly private. Enjoy the view of the house and park but do not trespass, turn left along the drive which leads to the bridge, and which winds to the right past a magnificent stand of redwood trees and comes out on the road.

Turn left along the road for about 200 yards and find the first field boundary on the right. Cross the ditch, keep the hedge on the left and walk along the headland of an arable field to go over the brow of the hill and eventually walk along the side of the woods on the right. The walk along the arable gives another splendid view of the house and the park. Enter the lane, turn right and follow the lane as it winds down the hollow into Combrook.

1. Combrook is a remote, rather quaint village which ranges on both sides of a deep valley through which winds the brook flowing from the lakes in Compton Verney Park. The village probably dates from the depopulation of Compton Murdak when the first Verney house was built in the middle of the 15th century. There are still a few old houses but most, like the church and the school, are of the Victorian Gothic Revival period. The church can only be described as an oddity, so unattractive it is worth examining as an extreme

example of bad taste in architecture. Even the angels which overload the base of the dumpy spire, seem to be trying to escape from it.
2. *Compton Verney appears in the Domesday Survey of 1086 as simply the manor of Compton held by Count de Meulan. In the 12th century it was granted by the Earl of Warwick to Robert Murdak from whom it took the name of Compton Murdak.*

In 1370 the estate was conveyed to Alice Perrers, the notoriously rapacious mistress of Edward III, and in 1440 the land was possessed by Richard Verney who built a fine house here, and the name Compton Verney first appears in the records in 1445. About 1540 Sir William Verney enlarged the house with stone from the ruined Hanley Castle which had been given to him by Henry VIII. (see Walk 21).

The ancestral home of the Verneys we see today was largely built in the 18th century by two great architects. The west range reputedly by Vanburgh, was built around 1714 in a rather severe classical style for Dr. George Verney, Lord Willoughby de Broke, who was also Dean of Windsor. Robert Adam's improvements after 1762 gave the facade a lighter, more attractive aspect by allowing the windows more importance, and by spacing them more widely. Seen from across the lake, which in itself is one of the most beautiful stretches of natural water created by Capability Brown, the facade of Compton Verney in pure Palladian style strikes the authentic note of the superb, urbane country seats which graced that wonderful Age of Elegance. Compton Verney remained with the Verney family until 1921.

Preamble
to Worcestershire Walks

It is foolhardy to attempt a summary of a county so varied and diverse as Worcestershire, small though it is in comparison with some. Nature and geology have distinctly endowed it and shaped the occupations of its people. The north is all industry, itself diverse, ranging from the heavy iron workings of the Black Country, to the glass works of Stourbridge and the carpet manufactories of Kidderminster. In the east Redditch is famed for its nails, needles and fish hooks. In these parts a network of canals sprang up to serve their industrial needs, leaving at Tardebigge a spectacular example of pick and shovel engineering, and at Stourport a gracious Georgian town as a legacy of the Industrial Revolution. The production of salt from the brine springs at Droitwich had long predated all this Victorian frenzy, consuming in the process much of the ancient forests of Feckenham and Malvern. From the skins of the forest animals sprang the beginnings of glove-making in the county town. On the alluvial soil of the Vale of Evesham spread the orchards of plum, pear and cherry whose spring blossoms still attract sightseers in their thousands. To the west is gentle farming country beloved of Elgar, its hop fields and orchards intimating its close kinship with its new and enforced administrative bedfellow.

With such marked differences of scenery, occupation and character, is it any wonder that its people differ so much in dialect and outlook? To hear a man from Stourbridge conversing with one from Pershore is to appreciate the gulf of experience that separates them, though they live but a few miles apart. These variation exemplify perfectly the splendid diversity of the Midland shires and indeed can occur from village to village.

Worcestershire is watered by the mighty Severn which was from early days the highway to the interior, being navigable to the trows right up to Bewdley, and bringing early prosperity to that elegant town where false pride later rejected the 'stinking ditch' of the canal. Further east the river Avon enters the county, meanders about in an unhurried way, and leaves again after enhancing the many villages and towns on its banks and richly endowing the fertile vales. In the west the Teme, smallest and most modest of them all, gives its name to many a place in the red clay lands where the Malverns, Bredon, the Ankerdines and the Abberleys dominate the scene. Unmistakably

Worcestershire is the vista from the Malvern ridge to the east, unmistakably Herefordshire is the markedly different prospect to the west. And through it all snakes the M5, replacing the Severn as the main north-south artery of communication.

Worcestershire's excursions into history have been brief but decisive. Saxon and Norman combined to establish under Wulfstan the beautiful cathedral which stands on the bank of the Severn. Decisive, brief and brutal the battle that took place at Evesham in 1265 resulting in the crushing of the beginnings of Parliament. Equally decisive in establishing the Commonwealth was Cromwell's 'crowning mercy' in 1651 — the battle of Worcester after which Charles Stuart was forced to flee the country.

A Plantagenet monarch loved Worcester and lies buried there. For the feckless Charles I it was the city 'faithful in war and peace' and it paid a heavy price, only to reap a reward for its loyalty later. The guildhall in the High Street with its elaborate and florid architrave, carrying statues of Charles I, Charles II and Queen Anne, with the head of Cromwell nailed by the ears, is the visible symbol of the overweening confidence, if not the gratitude of the restored Stuarts.

Rich in history and tradition, diverse in character and occupation, this part of the ancient kingdom of the Hwicce is small in compass, yet within its borders includes all the classical elements that compose the true West Midlands.

WALK 17
A WALK ALONG THE RIVERSIDE
AT EVESHAM.

O.S. Sheet No. 150 1:50,000 Worcester and the Malverns. Distance 2½ miles. Start point and car park Merstow Green. Grid Ref. 035444.

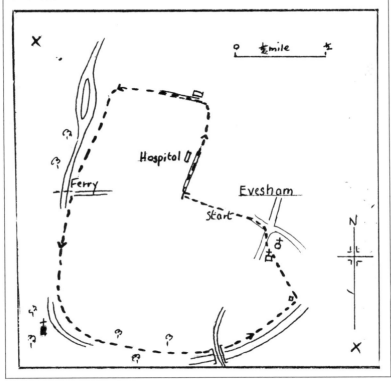

This pleasant, short walk is all on the level, following the river Avon in its wide loop from Glover's Island to Abbey Park, and taking in the most interesting historical features of the centre of Evesham. The paths are normally firm and dry although there may be some muddy patches in wet weather.

From the car park in Merstow Green walk along Bowne's Place, a narrow alley passing in front of a row of old cottages about fifty yards to the right of the fire station. Turn right into Bewdley Street

129

and cross to the right hand corner of another car park, to turn left into Littleworth Street which soon leads into Briar Close. Continue, passing the Hospital on the left, until the road forks beyond the Oddfellows Arms.

Take the left fork and then go to the left of Liley, Wright and Company's warehouses, where a finger post points left down a rough track. The path now goes across playing fields to reach the riverside. Turn left along the well-marked riverside path, passing the sports ground and eventually Hampton Ferry Cafe. The opposite bank, for much of the way is occupied by mobile homes which are all very neat and orderly. Past the ferry however it is a delight to see across the river fine willow trees, with the squat tower of Hampton church peeping above them.

Continue on the same heading past market gardens with fine crops of courgettes, parsley, leeks etc., and then past more playing fields, and on the riverside, numerous fishing stations manned by cheerful, optimistic anglers. Pass under Abbey Bridge when the path becomes tarmac and runs between a handsome avenue of trees. The Bell Tower is now in view on the slope to the left. Pass the boathouse of the Evesham Rowing Club and turn left away from the river, passing the paddling pool to aim for the old Abbey wall at the top of the slope.

To the left of the Bell tower the path runs along the left side of the old Abbey wall, goes behind the Almonry Museum to reach Abbey Road and so back to the car park in Merstow Green.

WALK 18
A WALK IN EVESHAM

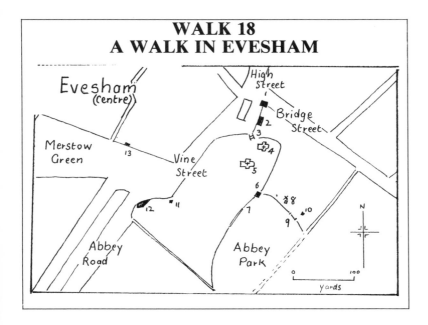

EVESHAM, E'SHAM, OR EVESSHAM — all three forms have appeared at various times in the past. Its ruined abbey, the last abbot, Clement Lichfield and Simon de Montfort, 'the father of English liberty', have all left their mark on the town. Nature has endowed it with its 'inexhaustible fertility' in the form of its rich alluvial clay so prized by growers, but so abhorred by ramblers when the rain has reduced it to a yellow, glutinous mess.

Evesham's once mighty abbey, a source of great prosperity to the town throughout the middle ages, owed its legendary origin to a vision of the Virgin vouchsafed to Eoves a swineherd, who at once communicated it to Ecgwin, Bishop of Worcester, who in turn was so moved he founded a monastery on the very spot where the vision had occurred. Ecgwin was the first abbot and died at Evesham in 717. The abbey grew in importance and wealth as a place of pilgrimage and with it the town, which even then had an important function as host to ecclesiastical tourists, just as it is today to the people of Birmingham and the Black Country, who come in search of the pleasures afforded by the river and park, or to take part in the angling contests, or the popular Regatta held every August Bank Holiday. The prize for the winner was once a silver replica of the

*Bell Tower, but alas this unique trophy disappeared without trace
some years ago. The Rowing Club still flourishes, the river is still
popular for boating and as in the Middle Ages Evesham attracts the
short-stay tripper, and this continuity is one of the features that
gives the town its distinctive appeal among Midland market towns.*

*The abbey's religious reputation was secure from its foundation,
but its abbots varied greatly in ability and dedication. Some were
grasping, self-indulgent, and contemptuous of their sacred charge,
preferring to squander the abbey's revenues and neglect the upkeep
of the buildings. One such was Robert Norreys, appointed by King
John against the advice of the Archbishop, Stephen Langton.
Norreys was a degenerate monk who had been imprisoned for past
misdeeds, and was described as 'puffed up, pompous, treacherous,
irreligious, a companion of females, and a lover of horses!' He was
only deposed after a long and disastrous term of office, by a special
Papal decree. Other abbots ably fulfilled all the requirements of
their saintly office, combining scholarship, piety and the administrative skills which were necessary in such a large religious
institution. Among them was Thomas de Marleberge who did much
to repair the ravages of Norreys.*

*The last and best known of the Evesham abbots wass Clement
Lichfield, a man of great piety and compassion, who maintained the
abbey with loving care and built the strikingly beautiful Bell Tower,
(6) a gem of the perpendicular style and surely one of the nation's
architectural treasures. It has twelve tiers of arcading, stepped
buttresses, an ogee walk-through, and is surmounted by eight
delicate pinnacles. Its sonorous chimes ring out over the town every
quarter hour, and every three hours it renders an old and well-loved
tune, 'Barbara Allen' being one of the favourites. The Tower sits
four-square on the hill above the river, mercifully spared from the
wreckage of the great abbey, to remind us of past glories. Its builder
lived long enough to see its completion and almost certainly
intended it to be at once a monument to himself, and a beacon to
approaching pilgrims.*

*Clement Lichfield seems to have been acutely conscious of his
own worth and importance almost to the point of being vain-
glorious, yet his reputation is safe because of his piety and his desire
to help his fellow men. He founded the town's first grammar school
in the building which is now the Working Men's Club in Merstow
Green. (13). Yet he could not forbear to have inscribed over the
entrance, in letters now just hardly decipherable, 'Orate pro anima*

Clematis Abbatis'. *The school continued in use until 1879 when it was refounded at the bottom of Greenhill as Prince Henry's Grammar School, by a charter of James I granted in honour of his eldest son.*

The good abbot also embellished the town's two churches with chantry chapels, again in his own honour. The one in All Saints, (4) where he is buried, has fan vaulting and side windows, one of which shows him carrying a model of the Bell Tower, and others depict Eoves, Bishop Ecgwin, and Simon de Montfort. All Saints was, and is, the church for the townsfolk, while its companion, St. Lawrence (5), was built specially for the pilgrims' use, and is now redundant though still beautifully maintained by the Redundant Churches' Trust. The Lichfield chapel here is smaller with a pendant boss and fan tracery. The exterior east end and wall of St. Lawrence are adorned with an array of Tudor carving and decoration displaying aspects of the stone-mason's craft. In the roof of the porch of All Saints is a carved oak pendant showing the symbols of the Passion.

Both churches are medieval with some 19th century restoration, and are built in soft, honey-coloured limestone with miniature towers and spires which would be dwarfed by their great neighbour the abbey. Together with the Bell Tower they lie just within the abbey precincts, and the whole enclave is now entered from the market place through the oldest surviving part of it, Abbot Reginald's Gateway, (3), restored in the last century, and with Norman arcading in the wall, and a timbered building above. The old vicarage, now the church office, completes the group.

It seems strange that a man of such vision as Clement Lichfield could not read the signs of the approaching disaster of dissolution. Broken and in despair he resigned, and retired to nearby Offenham where he died soon after, and was buried in All Saints Church in 1546. The last abbot, Philip Hawford was a mere appointee of Thomas Cromwell, created to surrender the abbey, a service for which he was rewarded with the deanery of Worcester.

The work of destruction was ruthlessly efficient, and for years the ruins of the abbey were used as a quarry, so that now all that remains is the curtain wall (7) in the churchyard which runs along the top of the slope in the Abbey Park to the gaunt and shattered 14th century entrance archway. (9). At its height the magnificent building had no less than 14 altars and was much larger than the abbeys at Pershore and Tewkesbury. With two churches in the town, the townsfolk did not have the option of purchasing part of the abbey as a place of

133

worship, as had happened in both Pershore and Tewkesbury. The Almonry survives, (12), and is now a museum of local interest situated in Vine Street — the name evocative of the vine husbandry practised by the monks on Clark's Hill. Nearby, beneath a shelter are the old town stocks. (11).

The abbey was at the height of its power in 1265 when the battle of Evesham took place outside its walls. Simon de Montfort was a popular hero invested with the aura of the father of English democracy, but it is most unlikely that he ever saw himself in that role, for Norman as he was, he would have regarded democracy as we know it as anathema, and a sure recipe for disorder. In some ways he anticipated the Wars of the Roses, for what interested him was baronial power as distinct from royalist power, a mere exchange of feudal rulers. It was for this purpose that he extended parliamentary franchise to include the emerging merchant classes, hoping thereby to gain a new power base for himself and his peers against the king.

At Lewes in 1264 he defeated the royalist army and took captive the hapless Henry III, whom he kept with him in his train. On 4th August 1265 Simon had crossed the river Avon at Kempsey and was awaiting the arrival of his son and more forces from his garrison at Kenilworth. Mounting the tower of the abbey early in the morning he saw an army approaching over Greenhill displaying his banners. It was a trick, for young Simon had been defeated at Kenilworth by Prince Edward. When the advancing army discarded the baronial banners and raised the royal ones, good soldier as he was, Simon de Montfort knew he was doomed, trapped in the great loop of the river, with Roger Mortimer holding the bridge and Prince Edward's army coming down on him. With the words 'Let us commend our souls to God, for our bodies are our enemies,' he prepared for his last battle.

Prince Edward, with the advantage of numbers and position, pushed down the hill and drove Simon's army back against the river. The fighting which took place in a terrible thunder storm, was most fierce with no quarter given by either side. Most of the Welsh recruits in Simon's army were slain as they tried to ford the river, whilst Simon and his knights were forced back into a narrow space. The captive king saved himself from his friends by raising his vizor and crying out. 'I am Henry of Winchester, your King.' Simon's son Henry went down, and finally the Earl himself. Fighting on foot and whirling his great sword above his head, he was at last felled by a

13th century Knight

blow from behind. With him perished 4000 others, including 18 barons and 160 knights.

The victors were ruthless in their vengeance. Simon's body was savagely mutilated and dismembered, the head, arms and legs being sent to London for public display. After the battle the monks collected his remains and buried them near the high altar. A granite cross (8) suitably inscribed, today marks the spot where he fell near the Bell Tower, and though he was never canonised, the presence of his body in the abbey gave fresh impetus to the pilgrimages and ensured continued prosperity to the town. As a postscript to the battle a memorial stone (10) brought from Simon's birth-place in France was set up in 1965 near the place of his death, in the presence of parliamentary and church dignitaries, to mark the 700th anniversary. The inscription commemorates him as a pioneer of representative government, which he was, though not for the idealistic reasons one might assume. Another stone which is set up on private ground at the top of Greenhill marks the site where the battle was joined, and from where Prince Edward launched his victorious assault on the beleagured Earl, whose name is still commemorated in the town by some street names.

Two recent books cast doubts on this, the long accepted version of the Battle of Evesham. Dr. David Cox does not believe that Greenhill was the site of the battle, and Dr. David Carpenter in his book 'The Battles of Lewes and Evesham', is sceptical of the numbers slain according to the chronicler, in view of the fact that so few remains have ever been discovered.

With the abbey's destruction came an inevitable decline in prosperity and a long period of comparative obscurity, but Evesham's saving grace lay, and still lies, in its marvellously fertile soil which can produce almost any vegetable crop. No doubt the monks had laid the foundations of good husbandry and horticultural practice, for certainly the area was, and still is, renowned for the excellence of its fruit and vegetables, the skill and hard work of the growers, and their prodigious thirst. Life carried on quietly enough until the coming of the canals and railways and the rapid growth of the Midlands' industrial centres created immense opportunities for the Vale's gardeners, who were now assured of a ready market near at hand for their produce. Nowadays the Vale seen from the surrounding hills gives the impression of being half submerged under water when the light shimmers on the acres of glass under which early lettuce, cucumbers and tomatoes are grown. In summer, luxury crops like asparagus are grown, but the staple crops are brussels in winter and plums and soft fruit in summer, when the town's markets are ceaselessly in use. Prior to the fruit comes the blossom, a great attraction and not to be missed on 'Blossom Sunday' when the Vale seems to be a mass of white blooms. It is also a time of much danger for the growers, for one night's frost can destroy the work and rewards of a whole year. Diversification of crops is widely carried on by means of a 'strip system', and though big growing organisations have moved in, there is still no lack of small growers eager to be first on the market with their produce.

Avoid Evesham and its traffic in the height of summer. Unless you intend joining in the fruit-picking, it is best to avoid the over-crowding in August when the plums are being harvested. At other times enjoy the amenities and the unusual flavour of the place, for there are not many like it. Some of the buildings are worth a careful look. Dresden House in High Street is Georgian and so named because of a doctor who lived there before he emigrated to Dresden in the late 18th century, and became famous as physician to Frederick the Great of Prussia. The 15th century Round House (1) in the Market Place was originally a merchant's house which was carefully restored in 1965 and is now a branch of the National Westminster Bank. The neo-Georgian Public Hall (2) is unpretentious and fits in well.

A link with the abbey is provided by the presence in the former Crown Hotel in Bridge Street of a well once used by the monks when entertaining visitors in the old hostelry. This fine house with court-yard and balcony above used to be a favourite with both townsfolk and tourists until dissolution of a kind overtook it too. A touch of more recent glamour came to the town in the last century when the family of the exiled Emperor of the French, who had assumed the title of the Duc d'Orleans, came to settle at nearby Wood Norton in 1872. The house remained in their possession until 1912, when it became for a time a preparatory school and is now a training school for the BBC.

Evesham does not overtly set out to attract the hordes of visitors that crowd the streets of its neighbours, Stratford and Warwick. It is not fixed in its past, though past it has indeed; it is a working town more interested in its current activities and the businesses which enable it to take care of the present and the future, without undue regard to what has gone before.

WALK 19
PERSHORE – TIDDESLEY WOOD – PERSHORE.

O.S. Sheet No. 150 1:50,000 Worcester and the Malverns. Distance 5 miles approx. Start point and car park off high street – Grid Ref. 950451.

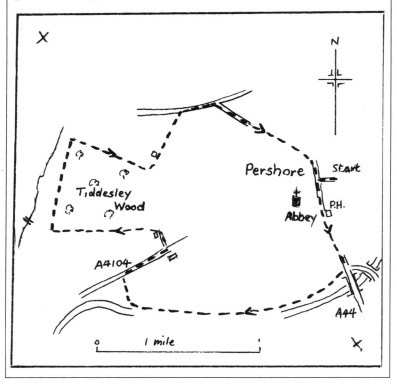

This walk begins with a stroll down the High Street to the Avon bridge, then crosses lush river meadows to the A4104 before entering Tiddesley Wood, a Nature Reserve set up with the help of the World Wild Life Fund. It then returns to Pershore along tracks and roads and is everywhere flat and easy, the only possible problem being muddy patches in the wood. 'The Angel Hotel' provides an ideal lunchtime rendezvous.

From the car park in the middle of the High Street walk left along the A44 for about ½ mile to reach a signposted footpath to Tiddesley Wood on the north side of the bridge. The 14th century packhorse bridge has been preserved alongside. The wide centre was restored after it had been destroyed by Royalists fleeing from the crushing defeat at Worcester on 3rd September, 1651. (See Walk 23). Follow the well-trodden path along the river bank, with a superb view of the graceful abbey tower across the flowery meadows.

'For, lo, the winter is past, the rain is over and gone;
The flowers appear on the earth; the time of the singing of the birds is come.' (Song of Solomon − 2, xii.)

On the sparkling May morning of our walk the bankside was thick with cow-parsley and charlock, presenting a most colourful and fragrant border to the sleepy Avon. In the distance across a river rose the splendid backcloth of Bredon Hill.

Charlock

The path follows the meandering river through rough pasture, along the edge of arable fields and market gardens, and through lush meadows, with stepstiles and sturdy wooden foot-bridges at regular intervals. As the river and the path approach the A4104, across the foot-bridge and over a stile, a path on the right leads to the road.

Turn right along the A4104 for about ¼ mile to find Tiddesley Wood Lane, a tarmac vehicle track on the left, and directly opposite a garden centre. At the top of the lane, at Woodman's Cottage, go over a stile and walk across sheep pastures to enter Tiddesley Wood. Look out for spotted orchids and white dog roses. Keep to the broad track and where tracks cross, keep straight ahead. Later when the main track forks, go to the right.

Suddenly at the top of a rise, Besford Court with its tall chimneys can be seen straight ahead. The Harewells, Lords of the Manor at Besford in the 15th century, built the house which was enlarged in the 20th century by a north country industrialist. The church at Besford is a quaint, timber-framed building with a bell turret, and contains two treasures, viz., an ancient rood-loft, which escaped the Tudor vandals, and a triptych illustrating the life and death of 15 year old Richard Harewell. There are also memorials to the Sebrights, successors to the Harewells. At the top of the rise just before a railed bridge find a stepstile partially concealed by under-growth and overhang on the right which gives on to a path skirting the edge of the wood. Follow this and if it is May enjoy the sight of the bluebells carpeting the wood, and the Malverns on the left rearing their huge bulk skywards.

Over another stile go right and with an orchard on the left, enter the edge of the wood, continuing through it for a few hundred yards to emerge on to a vehicle track. Turn left and passing through a wooden gate follow the track to the road. Go right uphill, and before turning right again at a '30' sign cast a glance behind for a last glimpse of the Malverns. Then go down the hill past houses with the Abbey tower in view, turn left at the bottom along Three Springs Road, and right at the main road junction to walk along the main street back to the park and the 'Angel'.

Pershore, from the Saxon 'pursh' meaning 'willow' is a most attractive town set in open country so that flowery meadows alongside the Avon seem to come right up to the High Street. It is also a remarkably intact Georgian town with numerous delightful houses of stone, brick and stucco in Bridge Street, many with Venetian windows, pillared porches with individual fanlights, splendid coach doorways and narrow alleys opening on to gardens with superb views of the river. Of special interest perhaps are the Midland and Barclay's banks, the former 'Three Tuns' Hotel with its cast iron veranda at the corner of the market place, and Perrott House built in 1760.

These Georgian facades however are an 'improvement' on the original buildings, masking their timber-framed construction which can be glimpsed in some of the coach entries and demonstrating the wealth and elegance of 18th century Pershore, whose prosperity was largely based on wool. The presence of numerous mills along the Avon banks, as at nearby Fladbury and Pershore itself, which were mainly used for fulling and preparing locally made cloth in medieval times, indicates the importance of the district in this regard. Indeed, the impression one gains in Pershore is that of quiet unhurried prosperity, nurtured originally by the Abbey and the pilgrims it attracted, then by the woollen industry, and finally by the growth and importance of the fruit and vegetable markets for which, along with Evesham, the place is justly famous. The traditions of good horticultural practice initiated by the monks are still maintained by local growers and further developed by the students of the nearby horticultural college. Both growers and students enjoy the advantages of the rich alluvial clay which produces bountiful crops and supports the numerous and varied orchards of fruit, especially the renowned Pershore plum, so excellent for jamming and preserving. The production of these crops however is not without its risks, and has given rise to the reply 'Pershore, God help us', supposed to have been given by a Pershore man when asked in a bad season of crop failure where he came from. It is also alleged that this remark was often misapplied by Evesham folk in the past as a condescending reference to the supposed fact that nothing ever happened at Pershore, but if this were ever true it is certainly not so today, for the town has a busy market, flourishing shops, a festival based on the Abbey, and extensive housing estates on the outskirts.

The early history of the Abbey was stormy. A community of secular canons established on the north bank of the river in 690 by Oswald the nephew of Ethelred, King of Mercia, was destroyed in a Danish raid in the 9th century. This was not quite the disaster that might be thought, as Saxon buildings were invariably of wood for the most part and unlikely to survive anyway. A similar fate again befell the place which was frequented by Odda whose chapel at Deerhurst has recently been discovered. In 972 the West Saxon ruler Edgar granted a charter to the Benedictines for a monastery at Pershore which was richly endowed with lands in Worcestershire and Gloucestershire and which also possessed valuable rights in the salt pans at Droitwich. Late in the 11th century the Benedictines began work in stone on the church which eventually, by the end of the 13th century, was probably the finest Benedictine building in the country rivalling its neighbours at Tewkesbury and Gloucester for size.

The monks dedicated their Abbey of the Holy Cross to St. Eadburga, patron also of the old church at Broadway, who after exhibiting signs of extraordinary piety as a child was placed in a convent and revered for her holiness. After her death, some of her bones were sent as a relic to Pershore and attracted pilgrims from far and wide for their alleged healing qualities. Her special little chapel on the south side of the nave was pulled down as unsafe along with the Lady Chapel in the 16th century, a form of needless vandalism which has not improved the appearance of the rest of the buildings.

Sadly, at the Dissolution in 1539, the town was unable or unwilling to buy and preserve the whole church and today only the tower and choir remain of the splendid medieval edifice. A window in the south aisle depicts the history and dissolution of the Abbey, showing a monk kissing the feet of one of Thomas Cromwell's commissioners in a most fawning and sycophantic manner. It probably represents the monk Richard Beesley who was so anxious to curry favour with the new order that he wrote to the commissioners describing the shortcomings of some members of the community of the Holy Cross — 'Now y wyle ynstrux your grace sumwatt of relygus men. Moncks drynk an bowll after collacyon till ten or XII of the clock, and cum to mattens as dronk as myss and sume at cardes, sume at dyss and at tabulles, sum cum to mattens begenynge at the mydes and sum when yt ys allmost done, and wold not cum ther so, only for boddly punnysment, nothyng for Godes sayck.' Even if all this were untrue it shows a house divided against itself, with some having their eyes firmly fixed on the main chance. Needless to say the Abbey did not escape and, one hopes, perhaps Beesley did not either.

What remains today is nonetheless magnificent though sorely truncated and shored up by huge buttresses. The superb lantern tower decorated externally with two bands of ball flowers floods the west end with light and is arguably surpassed only by that of Lincoln. The presbytery is similarly lofty and of superb proportions, with its recessed arches standing on slender pillars of clustered shafts topped with capitals displaying the most delicate

142

overhanging foliage. Above, the eye is carried to a most unusual and attractive feature – the triforium and clerestory merging in a single harmonious arcade. The perfect vaulted roof of the middle 14th century with its 41 huge carved bosses displaying the rich foliage of vine, oak and ivy includes one showing a face with open mouth known as 'The Shouting Man'. At the west end are the Hazelwood tombs and those of a cross-legged knight and a 14th century Abbot.

Across the way from the Abbey grounds is the deconsecrated church of St. Andrew which now serves the town as a community centre. It was built, mainly in 15th century work, because Edward the Confessor had seized many of the Pershore lands and houses to endow his new Abbey of Westminster, and the monks, understandably angry, were unwilling for the townsfolk, now technically Westminster tenants, to worship any longer in their Abbey.

WALK 20
ELMLEY CASTLE – BREDON HILL –
OVERBURY – ELMLEY CASTLE.

O.S. Sheet No. 150 1:50,000 Worcester and the Malverns. Distance – a.m. 4 miles, p.m. 4 miles. Grid Ref. 982411.

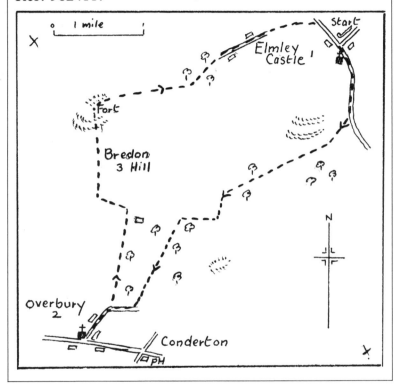

This is a most stimulating outing which includes a stroll through two charming villages, some rough walking up modest slopes, and, weather permitting, splendid views across the Severn Valley to the Malverns, and over the Vale of Evesham to the Cotswolds. The paths are well-marked and the going is firm, but there could be some muddy, slippery patches on the bridle-paths in the woods. Good, strong footwear is recommended here for all seasons.

144

A convenient parking place should be found near the village hall opposite the 'Queen's Head' Inn at the top of the wide village street. Go down the narrow lane opposite the inn, walk past the village's neat little cricket pitch, and continue on the road for about half a mile. Find a bridleway marker on the right-hand hedge opposite a farm track, and take this path, keeping the hedge on the left. Go through a gate with a gold crown and blue arrow waymarker, and follow the path which is directed to the left. After a few hundred yards turn right to pass over a plank bridge and come upon a waymarked stake. The path now leaves the tractor-marked trail and climbs quite steeply for a while up the hillside.

On the right is a mound which is all that remains of the castle built here by Robert Despenser in the 11th century. In 1540 John Leland observed carts carrying stones away from the ruins of the castle to repair the bridge at Pershore.

The twisting way through the spinney is well marked by blue arrows on the trees. Carry on uphill keeping the ditch well in sight on the left while the view widens splendidly behind. Reach a way-marked bridle-gate and continue to follow the direction given by the blue arrows through the woods. The path climbs steadily and can become rather rutted and muddy in places. Watch out for the marker at a junction of paths and pass an extremely venerable oak on the right with the familiar blue arrow on the post, close to a stone wall on the left. Continue upward through woods of ash and sycamore to reach the summit of the hill.

We now meet another track which runs roughly at right-angles. Ignore the direction pointed by the blue arrow, cross over the new track and go straight through a wooden gate, to walk ahead with the field fence on the left, and go through a second wooden gate. There are tall Scots pines marking the right side of a farm track. Follow the track and the line of trees to the right. Away to the right is a pine wood and a tall, unsightly column; monstrous, modern apparatus needed to improve our tele-communications. The path now skirts a pine wood on the left.

Just before a tarmac farm track is reached, turn left through a gate and continue with the pine wood on the left. Go through yet another gate and carry on alongside a stone wall with an arable field now on the right. Keep on the same heading going through several gates to cross over a farm drive. Aim for a wood directly ahead and when the edge of the wood is reached, turn left along the edge of an arable field to pass round a number of barns. The path now goes

Pheasants

along the side of a wood on the right, and on the left we found an immense field of unharvested flax where every few yards we seemed to disturb fat pheasant cocks uttering their ludicrous 'hot water bottle' alarm cry as they scurried along the path in front of us.

At the end of the wood turn left along a pleasant, narrow lane which leads down into Overbury. At the main road turn left for the 'Star Inn' and most welcome refreshments. Retrace steps to Overbury, and after visiting the church, go up the lane opposite the gates of the great house and walk left along the raised pavement. Turn left along a drive marked 'Private' but where there is a right of way, cross the cattle-grid and go steadily uphill on the tarmac drive through pleasant parkland and sheep-pasture.

The path now passes between woods where you may be fortunate enough to get a glimpse of shy fallow deer. The woods eventually give way to arable. Turn left through a gate and walk along a wide farm track which is edged with lofty beech trees, and beyond is a fine view across Overbury village to Dumbleton Hill. Go through a gate to enter lush meadows and keep ahead to pass by old, and sadly, rubbish-filled quarries on the left. Following the same heading reach an old barn surrounded by trees, and just beyond the barn turn right along a path, keeping the stone wall on the left and walk towards a coppice. Over a stepstile turn right and walk along a wide track between trees. Go through a metal gate and walk across rough pasture with a stone wall on the left – the rough hummocks of the Iron Ages Fort already appear on the right. Parson's Folly or Tower stands on a mound directly ahead. The view is now opened across the Severn Valley to the Malverns and beyond.

'Here on a Sunday morning
My love and I would lie,
And see the coloured counties,
And see the larks so high.'

(A.E.Housman)

From the Tower, walk on the old heading across the ancient trenches and ramparts of the hill fort, keeping the stone wall on the left to come upon a hunting gate. Do not go through the gate but turn right and walk across the rough pasture with the stone wall still on the left.

Through a gate keep on the same heading with a wire fence on the right. The high ridge now provides a striking view across the valley to Pershore with its mellow, golden, abbey tower. Reach the edge of a wood, (the telecom monster has now re-appeared ahead on the right), and turn left downhill keeping the wood on the right for a few hundred yards. At the end of the wood turn right down a gulley to follow the path through the quarries. Go through a metal gate and keep on the same heading downhill to cross a farm track and turn right for a few yards down a hollow way. Go through a metal gate to enter a short, overgrown gulley which soon enters a pleasant lane twisting steadily downhill, past neat, thatched cottages to return to the 'Queen's Head' at Elmley Castle.

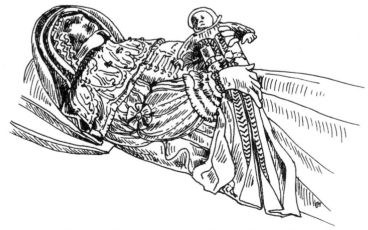

Detail of the Savage tomb in Emley Castle Church

147

1.   *Elmley Castle. This is a most attractive and intriguing village, nestling at the foot of Bredon Hill. The main street, which is so wide it has the appearance of a square and gives a natural focus to the village, has several fine houses in stone and half-timber, all splendidly maintained, while the stream which is neatly channelled down the east side of the street, adds a touch of extra charm.*

The church is entered through a 16th century porch, enlivened with a number of crudely carved stones of the Norman period which have been set into the wall at random. The chancel is largely 12th century and the remainder, nave and aisles are a mixture of 14th, 15th and 16th century work. The font support is 13th century and presents a most realistic carving of writhing dragons. The bowl is 16th century with elaborately carved sides showing the wounds of Christ, the Virgin's lily, the Prince of Wales' plumes, the arms of the Beauchamp and Savage families, and the rebus of the church's 16th century patron, John Brereton.

The Savage memorial dates from the reign of Charles I and shows effigies of Sir William Savage, his son Giles, Giles' wife Katherine holding a baby, while four children kneel in reverence at the feet of the main effigies. The monument is carved most delicately and crisply in fine alabaster. Opposite is the rather overpowering, blatant, Baroque monument to Thomas, Earl of Coventry, who married his housekeeper's niece in his dotage. The monument has a most elaborate pillared canopy which seems to threaten to push through the roof of the church. On either side are well carved figures of Faith and Hope. The inscription reads: 'Reader build thou thy tomb while yet thou livest, If Fortune hath not given thee a spouse.' The monument dates from the early 18th century and was placed in the church by the Earl's widow who later married into the Savage family. The Earl's successor had refused to have the monument in the family church at Croome on the grounds that the descent claimed for the Duchess on the inscription was alleged to be inaccurate, — 'she being of mean descent, the daughter of a turner.'

2.   *Overbury. This is a quiet, retiring but nevertheless attractive village built in stone. It was built almost entirely to suit the tastes of the Martin family who came to live in the Manor in 1723. When the old house was burnt down in 1738, John Martin, the banker, replaced it with the present, imposing Overbury Court. In the 19th century, the architect Norman Shaw was commissioned to 'prettify' the village, and the result of his efforts to produce rustic charm to order, may be seen in the lane to the north of the church, where he*

has provided a pleasant mixture of substantial estate cottages and several impressive individual buildings, including the Red House with its appealing Venetian windows.

The church has a commanding position and the churchyard is entered through a fine timber lych gate surmounting a flight of steps, and which now serves most sensibly as a war memorial. The tower of the late 15th century has curious gargoyles. The nave is Norman with the familiar massive piers, here surmounted by clumsy square capitals. The main item of interest is the Norman font which has an appealing shape, and the carving has escaped mutilation.

3.   Bredon Hill although no great height, (a thousand feet or so), nevertheless rises most dramatically above the flat, clay-bound country of the Vale of Evesham. From earliest times it must have offered farming men well-drained land facing the sun, which could be cleared more easily than the dense, marshy forests in the surrounding valleys.

About 200 years before the Roman invasion of Britain the hill was taken over by Iberian people who came up the Severn Valley from the west. They were herdsmen and farmers who were seeking fresh lands to graze and till, and they built, near the summit of the hill, a fortified village which looked west to the next high country, – the Malverns. Sometime before the Roman invasion the fort-village was sacked, probably by a neighbouring tribe, and when excavation was carried out here in 1937, a heap of about 50 dismembered skeletons was found in the main entrance to the fort.

WALK 21
UPTON-UPON-SEVERN — HANLEY CASTLE — UPTON-UPON-SEVERN.

O.S. Sheet No. 150 1:50,000 Worcester and the Malverns. Distance 3½ miles. Grid Ref. 852415.

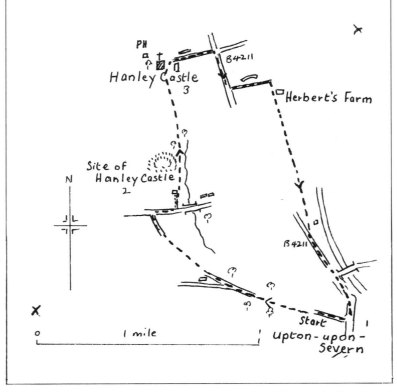

This is a delightful walk full of varied interest, along quiet lanes and well-marked paths, which can be enjoyed at any season.

From the car park behind the fire station in New Street, turn left and walk along Hyde Lane, a quiet, tree-lined road, which on the superb Spring morning of our walk was enlivened on each side with hosts of delicate, lavender coloured ladies' smock, which was often called cuckoo flower, because it appeared with the cuckoo every year.

'When daises pied and violets blue,
And lady-smocks all silver white,
And cuckoo buds of yellow hue
Do paint the meadows with delight!
                    (Love's Labours Lost. Act V, sc.iii)

Ahead now we have a clear view of the Malvern Hills as the lane winds alongside a stream lined on either bank with leaning willow trees. After about half a mile fork right where a handsome red brick farm stands on a slope to the left. Continue along the quiet lane, with the hedges now coloured with gorse in bloom, dark red flowering currant and here, weigela, to go past a neat, cream-coloured cottage. The lane winds right and on the left is an impressive house with a well-kept lawn and a pool complete with black swans! Go along the drive past the farm and through a metal gate find on the left the deep ditch and mound, all that remains of Hanley Castle. (The owner of the house is applying to have the footpath moved to the higher ground across the stream, but until permission is granted the right of way is along the drive. We would ask ramblers to pass through quietly and cause as little disturbance as possible.) The grassy slope rising from the ditch is bright with primroses, cowslips and ladies' smock.

Over a stile go through a kissing gate on the left and walk between tall hawthorn hedges at the side of an arable field. Hanley church, with tall trees alongside, stands out boldly ahead. Go through another metal gate into the churchyard. The church of St. Mary and St. Gabriel is an odd mixture of stone and old brick, while the tower seems out of place standing on the south side between the nave and the chancel. Inside, the west window has a quaint doom showing St. Michael weighing souls on Judgement Day, and in the chapel is a memorial to Captain Edmund Lechmere who fell to a musket shot from a French privateer in1703.

The High School alongside the church is on the site of the Grammar School founded in 1326 and restored in 1733. Hanley is a pretty, well-cared for village with a tiny inn and a number of attractive, timber-framed houses.

From the church, turn right along the lane to reach the B4211. Turn right here for about ¼ mile and then turn left along Quay Lane and walk past Longcroft Close to find a footpath sign on the right. Follow the track around the farm buildings and the familiar tower and cupola of St. Peter and St. Paul's old church at Upton come

The Church Tower and bridge, Upton-on-Severn

into view ahead. We now have a splendid view of the whole range of the Malvern Hills away to the right.

Go through a metal gate and follow a well-marked track across an arable field to find a stile in the left-hand corner near to the river. Continue along the path close to the river and turn right past a chicken house to come out on the drive to Pool House. At the end of the drive join the B4211 again and walk into Upton.

1. Upton-upon-Severn is a most attractive, ancient market town lying low in the meadows on the west bank of the Severn, and as yet relatively unspoilt by the familiar clutter which goes with modern development. It has a superb backcloth in the nearby Malvern hills, while the approach from the east across the modern metal bridge, with the slender 14th century tower topped by a Baroque coppered dome standing above the river, gives it a distinct continental air.

By the time of the Domesday Survey in 1086, Upton was already a thriving town, a junction of roads, an important river-crossing, and a busy port for river traffic, transporting timber, salt, wine, and pottery from Hanley Castle. The town's prosperity grew with the increase in river commerce in the 16th and 17th centuries when inland roads were still inadequate. During this period there was a considerable development of houses and warehouses around the original settlement. The symbol of this growth was the two-masted trow which used sail and tide up from Bristol, but which relied on gangs of bow-hauliers to pull the heavy, laden vessels up-river.

The bow-hauliers were often an unruly community much given to drinking and brawling, and prone to riot if they felt their well-being was being threatened. Because the river banks were infested with pirates and brigands, large gangs of bow-hauliers were needed to haul the trows and protect the cargoes. When in the 19th century the trow-masters proposed to employ horses to haul the vessels up-river, the riot of the bow-hauliers in Upton was so fierce and prolonged, that in 1832 a regiment of Scots Greys was sent from Worcester to disperse the unruly mob and restore order.

Upton did not then present the neat, dignified appearance it has today. Local records of the 17th and 18th centuries reveal evidence of the most disgusting squalor which prevailed. 'We do order yt no Cowes Bellys be emptied in the streets by ye butchers.' 'No person within the Berrow shall suffer any Mixon (dunghill) to lye above the pace of 16 days.' There were several huge sawpits in the High Street, pigsties in every side street, and even on the bridge, and a stinking gumstool or ducking pond at the end of New Street. The plague ravaged the town in 1665 and there were recurrent outbreaks of smallpox and cholera throughout the 18th and early 19th centuries.

With the arrival of the railway in the 19th century Upton's river trade fell off and the town began to assume its modern, charming, genteel air.

Celia Fiennes visited Upton in 1697: 'Hence to Upton where we pass on a large bridge over the fine river Severn, which runs from Worcester and to Gloucester, Shrewsbury and to Bristol, where it runs into the sea. I think this river does not ebb and flow so farre into the land.' (Illustrated Journeys of Celia Feinnes. Ed. Christopher Morris. p. 230) She was quite mistaken however, for in her day the river was still uncontrolled and the Severn bore could flood the countryside for 30 miles around.

'See how this river comes one cranking in,
And cuts me from the best of all my land,
A huge half moon, a monstrous cantle out!
I'll have the current in this place dammed.'
(Henry IV, Part 1, Act III, sc.i.)

In 1483 the 'Army of Edward V' led by the Duke of Buckingham was unable to cross the wooden bridge at Upton because of severe floods. (See Walk 27).

Until the 14th century the river had to be crossed here by a ferry, and the bridge built in 1480 was a flimsy wooden structure which was constantly in need of repair. A stone bridge was erected in 1593 but was already in a ruinous condition by 1606, and a sturdier bridge was at last built in 1609 with stone brought down from Hanley Castle. Broken in 1643 it was repaired only to be rendered impassable again in 1644, and was finally destroyed by the Scots army in 1651. When Prince Charles and his army of 'Cavaliers and Puritans' marched towards Worcester in the late summer of 1651, an advance force of about 500 led by Colonel Massey occupied Upton to hold the bridge and prevent the crossing of any Parliamentary forces.

The bridge was already in ruins from previous assaults and the Royalists seem to have been too confident of their security in the town. Early in the morning of the 28th of August, a company of Parliamentarians led by Colonel Lambert advanced quietly along the east bank of the river, and a small party was able to cross by a plank which the Royalist guards had carelessly left across the breach in the bridge. The Parliamentarians then barricaded themselves in the church while the main force was crossing the river by the ford to the south of the town.

The Royalists, now fully alerted, made a furious attack on the church but were held off by musket fire from the windows. The diversion gave Lambert's main force time to cross the river and to engage the enemy in hand to hand fighting in the streets. Taken by surprise and utterly confused, the Royalists fled to join their main army at Worcester.

A bridge of four spans was built in 1843, and that was swept away in the severe floods of 1872. A swing bridge was built which remained until the present cast iron bridge was erected in 1939.

Today Upton is a treasure house of domestic architecture from the 16th to the 19th century, all most carefully and lovingly preserved. Across Church Street, opposite the Bell Tower are two cottages, numbers 16 and 18, which are superb examples of timber-framed provincial houses of the late Elizabethan period. Most intriguing are the carpenters' marks clearly visible near the joints of the beams, which were used to assist in the work of assembling the timbers on the site. Walk along Church Street and across the road at the east end of High Street stands the 'Anchor Inn' which dates *from the early 17th century. The gable end which is now a shop, was once a tea exchange, and the date '1601' appears in the plaster of the gable above.*

On the west side of High Street the chemist's shop is an early 18th century building with a Venetian window above the shop. Opposite, Lloyds' Bank is an early 19th century building with attractive three-light bar windows, and a neat, moulded door-case. Across the street the 'White Lion' Hotel may be said to dominate the Hight Street. An Elizabethan building with a mid-18th century, three-storeyed frontage which is divided into bays by bold, fluted pilasters. A large porch projects over the pavement and is supported by Doric columns, and above the large white lion with its golden mane looks out over the street.

During the great coaching era of the late 18th and early 19th centuries the 'White Lion' was a popular coaching inn and features as 'the Inn at Upton' in Henry Fielding's novel 'Tom Jones', written in 1749. At the top of the building the Wild Goose Room, allegedly the scene of the episodes described in the novel, is beautifully preserved with its fine oak timbers intact. For a more leisurely and fuller itinerary of this entrancing town we recommend 'Upton Walkabout' (an illustrated guide to Upton's historic town centre and riverside.) by J. D. Wallis.

The Bell Tower with its curious hexagonal lantern and cupola is all that remains of the medieval church of St. Peter and St. Paul. It was seriously damaged in the Civil War skirmish in August 1651. In 1754 a new nave was built in the classical style, and in 1770, when the spire was considered unsafe, it was replaced by the wooden lantern. The 15th century nave was pulled down in 1937.

2. John Dee who held the rectory at Upton-on-Severn for more than fifty years in the reign of Elizabeth I, was born in London in 1527 and was educated at St. John's College, Cambridge. In 1546 he was one of the first fellows appointed to Trinity College founded by Henry VIII. The following year he was in the Low Countries conferring with learned men on astronomy. In 1550 he was lecturing in Paris on mathematics and physics, and in 1551, returned to England he was granted a pension of a hundred crowns which he exchanged for the rectory of Upton-on-Severn, where he was presented in 1553.

On the accession of Mary Tudor, because he was known to have corresponded with the Princess Elizabeth at Hatfield House, Dee was confined in Bishop Bonner's prison, charged with attempting to destroy the queen by magic. With the accession of Elizabeth in 1558 he was released and taken into the Queen's service, although he failed to secure any lucrative appointment, and in 1562 in depair he went to Antwerp, planning to publish his works on mathematics and astrology.

In 1564 he was in England again earnestly soliciting profitable employment from the government. He had no success although he seems to have kept the queen's favour. She promised him rewards and when he fell ill in 1571, she sent two of her physicians to attend him. In 1575 she visited his house in Mortlake, where he showed her his crystal ball and explained its use to her. Later we find him explaining to the queen the appearance of a new comet and undertaking to prevent any mischief befalling her from the discovery in Lincoln's Inn Fields of a wax effigy of her majesty with a pin piercing the breast. In 1578 Dee was again travelling abroad to consult learned physicians on the state of the queen's health, and in 1584 he was directed to make the necessary calculations for England to adopt the Gregorian calendar promulgated from Rome. His work was to be of no avail however when the bishops advised against the change on the grounds that it had emanated from Rome.

Dee was now spending more time looking into his crystal ball where he claimed he could see spirits and from which he could hear voices. His activities inevitably aroused the fear and anger of the mob who believed he was consorting with devils, and in 1583 they broke into his house and destroyed most of his furniture and burnt his books. At the same time his reputation as a magician and astrologer interested some in high places in Europe. In 1585 he was entertained by the King of Poland and in 1586 the Emperor Ivan the Terrible invited him to settle in Russia, offering him a pension of £2000, an offer which he refused.

Throughout much of his weird life John Dee was seeking the philosopher's stone which men believed could turn base metals to gold. He once sent Queen Elizabeth a small gold disc which he claimed to have made from part of a brass warming pan. Meanwhile his incessant appeals for preferment were invariably met with promises which were never fulfilled, and eventually he was compelled to accept the grant of the wardenship of Manchester College, where he arrived with his wife and family in 1596. Here he lived for some years on bad terms with the fellows of the College who accused him of poor management and of haughty behaviour.

With the death of Elizabeth I in 1603 he no longer had any friends in high places. The new King James I had written a learned work on witchcraft and sorcery, subjects which filled him with dread, and he was forewarned about the famous necromancer who was known to be 'an invocator of devils.' In 1604, in a poor state of health John Dee resigned his post at Manchester College and returned to Mortlake where he spent his remaining days in miserable poverty. He died in 1608 and was buried in the chancel of Mortlake church.

According to John Aubrey, (Brief Lives), John Dee 'had a very fair, clear sanguined complexion, a long beard as white as milk. A very handsome man, he was a great peacemaker; if any of his neighbours fell out, he would never lett them alone till he had made them friends. He was tall and slender. He wore a gowne like an artist's gowne, with hanging sleeves, and a slitt. A mighty good man he was — the children dreaded him because he was accounted a conjurer.'

(Letters by Eminent Persons, Vol II, pp 310–315)

John Dee produced 79 works on a great variety of subjects, mostly related to mathematics, physics, alchemy, astronomy and astrology. Few were actually printed.

3. Hanley Castle was built close to the right bank of the river Severn by King John in 1210. Assize Courts were held in the castle in 1211, and the King stayed there in November 1213. Like most of the Plantagenet kings John was an ardent devotee of the chase and according to the chronicler Holinshed, was always 'in a right merry humour' when engaged in hunting, and 'thought it scoffery to pursue fallow deer with hounds, but tired them out with his own travel on foot.'

Henry III gave the castle to Gilbert de Clare who married Joan of Acre here. Gilbert as Lord of Hanley Castle was also given government of Malvern Chase with sole power to issue the royal grant to privileged persons to hunt in the forest, and these were forbidden to exercise their privilege before and after any royal hunt so that 'the wild beasts might not by any means be disquieted of their rest and peace,' When Gilbert's authority over the Chase was challenged by the Bishop of Hereford, a bitter, violent quarrel ensued. (See Walk 22).

In the 15th century Hanley Castle passed to Richard Beauchamp, Earl of Warwick, through his marriage to Isabel Despenser who was descended from Gilbert de Clare. Richard Neville, Earl of Warwick, known as the Kingmaker, succeeded to the Beauchamp estates and used the castle often as a hunting lodge, and later during the

157

unsettled times of the Wars of the Roses, as a refuge for his wife and children. Through his marriage to Anne Neville, Hanley Castle came to Richard Duke of Gloucester, later Richard III, and it was possibly here and not in the Tower, that his younger brother George, Duke of Clarence, was drowned in a butt of malmsey wine.

> *'Take that, and that: if all this will not do,*
> *I'll drown you in the malmsey-butt within.'*
>
> *(Richard III, Act 1, sc.iv.)*

Sadly, Clarence's son Edward was also to die in Hanley Castle when his uncle Richard became king.

In the reign of Henry VII the castle was allowed to fall into decay and by the 16th century was in ruins. In 1540 John Leland described it as much dilapidated: 'Hanley is an uplandische towne. The Castelle standeth in a Park at the West Parte of the Towne. Syr John Savage and his Fauther and grandfauther lay much aboute Hanley as Keepers of Hanley. The Erles of Gloster were owners of this Castel and lay much there.'

> *(Itinerary — p.70)*

Henry VIII gave the ruin to Sir William Compton who pulled it down and carted off the stone to enlarge his house at Compton Verney in Warwickshire. (See Walk 16). What remained was largely used in the rebuilding of Upton bridge in 1608–9, and the remains of the gateway tower were finally demolished to provide stone for another bridge at Upton in 1795.

4.   The quiet idyllic village of Hanley Castle was once the home of Edmund Bonner, (1500–1569), who was born in a tiny cottage at the bottom of Quay Lane. He was the natural son of George Savage, later rector of Daveham in Cheshire. His mother later married Edward Bonner or Boner, a sawyer of Hanley Castle and young Edmund was probably educated in the local grammar school. Later he studied at Pembroke College, Oxford, where he graduated as a bachelor of canon and civil law and was ordained.

In 1529 he became chaplain to Cardinal Wolsey and after Wolsey's fall, he found favour with Thomas Cromwell, the King's secretary. In 1532 Bonner was sent to Rome to plead Henry VIII's case for a divorce from his queen, Catherine of Aragon. Bonner was also sent to appeal to Pope Clement against the king's excommunication following his bigamous marriage to Anne Boleyn, a request which greatly annoyed the pontiff, who folded and unfolded his handkerchief in evident agitation, 'which', wrote Bonner, 'he never doth but when he is tickled to the very heart with great choler.'

Bonner continued in the king's service and was sent on a number of diplomatic missions in France, Germany and Italy. In 1538 he was inducted Bishop of Winchester and appointed ambassador at the court of Francis I where his overbearing manner and unbridled language, managed to provoke that most courteous of sovereigns. In 1539 Bonner was rewarded by his appointment as Bishop of London and in 1542 went as ambassador to the court of the Emperor of Germany.

On the accession of young Edward VI in 1549 Bonner fell foul of the King's Council for his refusal to enforce the use of the new Book of Common Prayer. He was deprived of his see and committed to the Marshalsea prison, where he remained until the accession of Mary in 1553, when Bishop Ridley was dismissed and Bonner became once more Bishop of London. He set about restoring the catholic religion in England with burning zeal, beginning a series of such savage persecutions of protestants that he shocked the Spanish ambassador.

When Elizabeth I succeeded in 1558 Bonner was allowed to retain his see, although it was observed that the queen looked upon him coldly, and at the coronation refused him her hand to kiss. Later he refused to take the oath of Supremacy and was confined once more in the Marshalsea prison where he died in 1569.

Edmund Bonner was, beyond doubt, justly feared and hated in London. He was however an able, quick-witted lawyer, although reputedly argumentative and often ill-tempered. Whether he was the cold-blooded monster who gloated over the cruel torture of his victims, as portryaed by George Fox in his Book of Martyrs, is highly disputable.

WALK 22
A WALK ALONG THE HEREFORDSHIRE BEACON

O.S. Sheet No. 150 1:50,000 Worcester and the Malverns. Distance 4½ miles approx. Start point and car park — Wynd's Point, junction of A449 and B4232.

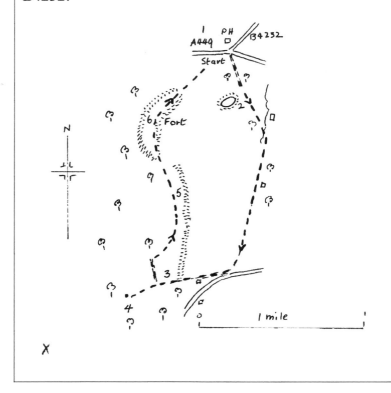

The Malvern Hills have about thirty miles of footpaths which offer almost an infinite variety of rambles. We have chosen a short walk suitable for any season, which provides splendid vistas, east across the Severn Valley to Bredon Hill and the Cotswolds, west across the hills and dales of Herefordshire to the rugged mountains of Radnor and Brecknock. The paths are well-marked and generally mud-free, the climbs are fairly gentle. Throughout the year these hills provide a feast of colours, but in summer the colours run riot with golden gorse, purple loosestrife, pink willow-herb, honeysuckle, foxgloves, and here and there on the heath, the delightful, delicate blue of patches of harebells.

From the car park take the tarmac lane which leads down the hill through pleasant woods below the towering Herefordshire Beacon. Soon the track passes to the left of a small reservoir which provides Malvern with its pure, sparkling water. Carry on past the reservoir where the rough path descends quite steeply, and bears slightly left. After a few yards, where the paths fork, go right and climb steadily along the side of the wooded slope. The way now levels and then drops gently down, and where it divides once more, go right, to cross a tiny brook and climb again as the path enters rough pasture. The slope to the right is covered with tall bracken in the summer.

The path now joins a farm track. Go through a gate, pass the farm and continue along the tarmac drive which runs alongside a wood on the left. When the drive turns sharply left at the beginning of the Common, keep straight ahead on the springy, grassy track which runs on the same heading at the foot of the hill. On the right we are now aware of the steep eastern slopes of the Beacon. When the path reaches a metal road turn right and then follow the left-hand tarmac lane which soon goes past a white cottage with a red-tiled roof, nestling in a dip below the road.

The quarry at the foot of Swinyard Hill appears ahead. Go to the left of the deep pool at the bottom of the quarry, bear slightly left, then turn sharp right to follow a rough, stony track which climbs steadily through the woods for about ¼ mile. At the top of the rise when the way leaves the woods, go through a gate, and, to visit the obelisk, follow the well-marked track on the same heading for another ¼ mile.

Return to the gate and turn sharp left to follow the path which leads past a white cottage and through a gate on the right. After about 100 yards go over a stile on the right and turn left along a rough cart track which leads through the woods to Swinyard Hill. The track is deeply rutted, and in wet weather could become rather muddy. It lasts for only a short distance however, and when the woods give way to the open hillside take the path on the right which climbs up to the crest of the hill and immediately opens up a splendid panoramic view east and west.

Go left along the ridge to reach Giant's Cave or Cutter's Cave.

Harebell

From the cave continue on the sane heading along the ridge and climb the narrow path which leads into the Iron Age Fort known as British Camp, which at 1395 feet is the highest point in the Malvern Hills. The path continues across the ancient ramparts and entrenchments to descend quite steeply to the car park.

1. The Malvern Hills are pre-Cambrian and amongst the oldest hills in the world. They rise so suddenly and steeply above the lush, flat country through which the river Severn meanders, as to dominate it completely. The hills change their appearance most dramatically according to the light and the weather. On a dull, overcast day they stand out starkly like a range of distant peaks; on a bright summer day they appear as gentle foothills basking in the sunshine. With snow on their flanks in winter they are at their most impressive and forbidding: with the coming of rain they magically take on a deep, blue tinge, and seem to have moved further away.

Celia Fiennes, writing in 1696 was greatly impressed. 'Here we enter into Worcestershire and ascend Maubon Hills or as some term them the English Alps − a ridge of hills dividing Worcestershire and Herifordshire and was formerly the line dividing England and Wales, Heriford, Shropshire etc. − they are at least 2 or 3 miles up and are in Pirrimidy fashion on the top; I rode upon the top of the highest, from whence could discern the country above 40 miles round, and none hills but what appeared like Burrows or Mole Hills;

these being so high nothing could limitt the eye but distance.'
(Illustrated Journeys of Celia Fiennes, 1685 — 1717.
Edited Christopher Morris, p.64.)
The A449 today follows the route of what was in early times, the
only pass through these hills. From Roman times the road was a
'saltway' along which salt was carried on packhorses from
Droitwich to settlements in South Wales. Through the pass at
Wynd's Point the road followed the ridgeway south-west across
what is today the park of Eastnor Castle. The car park at the
junction of the A449 and the B4232 is run by the Malvern Hills
Conservators, a body set up in 1884 to protect the area for the better
enjoyment of the public. A small charge is made for parking.
2.   The reservoir which nestles so naturally in the fold at the foot of
the Beacon was opened in 1895 by Princess Mary of Teck, the
consort of the Duke of York, later George V.

Water from so called holy wells in the hills had gained a
reputation for exceptional purity and curative qualities by the 17th
century. The diarist John Evelyn who walked on the Beacon on the
1st August, 1654 and declared that it provided 'one of the goodliest
vistas in England,' also wrote of the Malvern waters, 'they are said
to heale many infirmities, as Kings-Evil, Leprosie, etc., sore eyes.'

In 1757 Dr. John Wall published 'Experiments and Observations
on the Malvern Waters 'in which he described the beneficial effects
of taking Malvern water on patients in Worcester infirmary. John
Wall was born at Powick in 1708, the son of a Worcester tradesman.
He attended King's School, Worcester and was elected scholar of
Worcester College, Oxford. He took a degree in medicine at St.
Thomas's Hospital and set up practice as a doctor in Foregate Street
Worcester, where he gained some reputation as a good, practical
physician. Following the publication of his book, he worked
assiduously to promote Malvern water and in eighteen years trans-
formed an unknown village into a popular health resort.

By the 19th century taking the waters at Malvern had become
popular among the well-to-do, and celebrated visitors to the town
included Princess Victoria, her mother the Duchess of Kent, W.E.
Gladstone, Charles Dickens, Thomas Carlyle and Florence
Nightingale. Malvern Water is still widely 'taken' today from super-
market shelves; bottled by 'you know who' it vies in popularity with
Perrier Water and others.

Dr. Wall also became deeply involved in the porcelain works at
Worcester, (See Walk 23); in later life he suffered severely from

163

gout, a condition which no amount of Malvern water would relieve. He went to Bath to try the treatment advocated there, and died on 27th June, 1776 aged 69.

3. Gullet Quarry at the foot of Swinyard Hill provides an excellent illustration of the geological structure of the Malvern Hills. To the right of the sheer face are pre-Cambrian rocks laid down about 1000 million years ago. To the left are the more recent Silurian rocks formed some 400 million years ago. About 40 million years previously the whole area lay deep under the sea and the lower layers of sandstone we can see, were once part of a vast beach.

4. The obelisk, for all its 90 feet, seems quite dwarfed by the massive grandeur of the hills behind it. It was built in 1812 as a memorial to the members of the Somers family who seem to have been singularly unfortunate in the wars in which they engaged. Despite the notice to remind visitors that it is ' a memorial to the dead and should be respected as such', the monument is badly defaced by graffiti.

The west side commemorates John Lord Somers, Baron of Evesham, Lord High Chancellor in the reign of William III, and President of the Council in the reign of Queen Anne. He is best remembered for his defence of the Seven Bishops who, having dared to petition James II against the second Declaration of Indulgence in April 1688, were arrested, charged with seditious libel and committed to the Tower of London. Somers as their counsel in the trial, maintained that the petition was neither seditious, as it had been presented in private, nor a libel, since every subject had the right to petition the sovereign against a grievance. The jury acquitted the bishops amidst widespread popular rejoicing.

The south side commemorates the Lord Chancellor's nephew, James Cocks who died in 1758 in one of the 'nuisance raids' against the French coast which were planned by the Elder Pitt to keep French forces engaged in France, and so relieve Great Britain's ally, Frederick the Great, who was in danger of being overwhelmed by French, Austrian and Russian forces in Germany. Cocks was one of more then 2000 men killed in the raid which was condemned in Commons by Pitt's adversary Henry Fox as 'breaking windows with guineas.' The north side commemorates Edward Charles Cocks, son of the Lord Somers who built the monument, who lost his life in the Peninsular War in 1812, in a desperate and futile attack on the fortress of Burgos. After a series of attacks which cost the lives of 2000 soldiers, Wellington abandoned the assault on the fortress.

5.   Giant's Cave or Cutter's Cave is in fact an obvious man-made hollow of quite modest proportions which has been hewed into an outcrop of volcanic rock. It has been described as a medieval hermit's dwelling, a shepherd's shelter, and tradition has linked it with the fugitive Owen Glendower. There is no written record of its origin or use, nor do we know anything of the mysterious Cutter.

Above the cave on the ridge can be seen the remains of a rampart and ditch which were built in 1287 by Gilbert de Clare, the fiery 'Red Earl of Gloucester'. In ancient times the area was one huge, dense forest. In the 13th century the monastic chronicler William of Malmesbury describes the region as 'a vast wilderness', and even as late as 1540 John Leland maintained 'it is bigger than either Wire or Feckenham Forests, and it occupieth a greate parte of Malvern Hills.' Saxon kings hunted there and the Normans proclaimed it a royal forest governed from the castle at Hanley.

When Gilbert de Clare married Joan d'Acre the daughter of Edward I, as part of the wedding dowry he was granted the royal forest which now became known as Malvern Chase, since no subject could possess a forest. The hot-tempered Earl was soon involved in a bitter quarrel with the Bishop of Hereford who had also been granted hunting rights over the Chase, and had a hunting lodge at Colwall on the west side of the Hills. The Earl contested the Bishop's claim at law and when the judges decided in favour of the ecclesiastic, de Clare reconstructed an ancient earthwork on the crest of the ridge and placed on top a palisade of sharpened stakes to prevent deer from straying west into the Bishop's territory. Until recently the Red Earl's Dyke, also known as the Shire Ditch, marked the boundary between Worcestershire and Herefordshire.

On the slopes below this ridge, William Langland the 14th century poet is said to have been inspired to write 'The Vision of Piers Plowman'.

'In a May morning on Malvern Hills
A strange thing befell me, a fairy vision me thought,
I was weary with wandering and went me to rest,
Under a broad bank beside a stream.'

Langland is rather a shadowy figure who may have been born near Ledbury in 1332, may have been educated at Malvern Priory, and indeed may have written the poem.

6.   British Camp. These earthworks arguably represent the most impressive Iron Age fortress in Great Britain. The lower rampart

has a circumference of almost two miles, and the whole stronghold covers an area no less than forty-five acres. The huge entrenchments which are remarkably well-preserved, are from 6 to 12 feet deep, and in some places measure 30 feet across. The concentric lines of the ramparts lead quite evenly upwards to the citadel which was defended by a deep ditch and a high, stout wall. This part, it is believed, was completed about 200 BC.

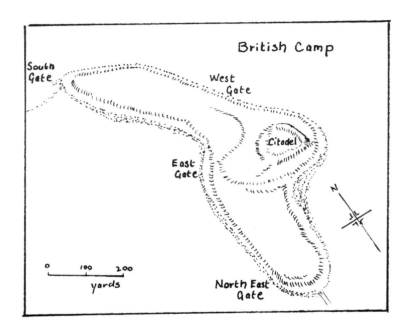

The hill itself presents a daunting, steep natural fortress, and when the walls were intact, it must have appeared impregnable in ancient times, when it would have given cover to many thousands of men. Commanding the only way through the hills it was probably a permanent fortress for hundreds of years before either Britons or Romans used it and enlarged the fortifications. Tradition has it that it was the site of Caractacus' brave stand against the Roman legions of Osterius Scapula. Under Caractacus' leadership, we are told, the Britons put up a stern fight but eventually had to yield, when Caractacus fled north to take refuge among the Brigantes, whose Queen Cartimondua finally betrayed him to his enemies.

WALK 23
A WALK AROUND THE ANCIENT CITY OF WORCESTER

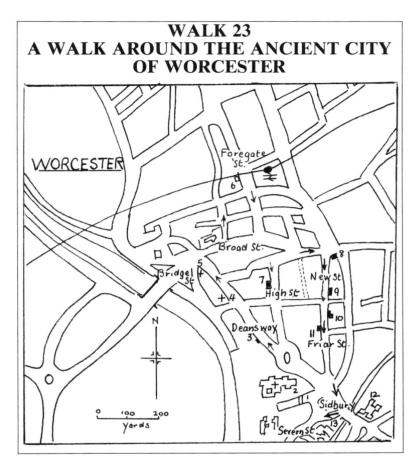

Today Worcester suffers from its position as a key crossing of the river Severn. The provision of a second bridge south of the city has done little to relieve the traffic congestion in the centre. New roads, roundabouts and car parks seem to dominate the area, and give the impression of a majestic medieval cathedral marooned in a wilderness of ceaselessly moving automobiles.

The itinerary begins at the Edgar Tower (1) built in the reign of King John as the entrance to the castle, of which nothing remains today. The fine gateway gives access to the cathedral close. Enter the cathedral by the north door, (2) and walk through the east side of the cloisters which are mainly 14th century, although the outer walls are

part of the original Norman church. Of particular interest in the cloisters is the squint in the piers of the inner wall which would have given a clear view into the carrels occupied by the monk-scribes.

From the cloister-walk a doorway opens into the chapter house with a single central pillar suporting the roof. Built in 1130 it became the prototype of later polygonal chapter houses built in England. Close by is a slype which is now used as a refreshment room, but which in the days of the monastery was a covered passageway from the abbot's lodging into the cathedral, and was probably used also as the monks' common room and warming room. The walls are lined with piers taken from the old Saxon cathedral of St. Oswald.

The nave presents a curious mixture of Transitional and Decorated styles of church architecture. The five eastern bays date from the 14th century, the two western bays were built about 1170 after the early Norman nave had been destroyed by fire in 1113. The marriage of the two styles cannot be described as entirely happy. Disasters continued to visit the church. In 1176 the central tower collapsed, in 1202 another fire brought more damage, and in 1222 a violent storm destroyed most of the Norman choir.

A new choir was begun in 1224 and was to produce one of the best examples of Early English architecture to be found in England. In particular the triforium provides one of the most delightful and eye-catching innovations of this great period of English church building.

Here each bay contains a pair of arches beautifully moulded and sub-divided, with sculptures in the tympanum above each sub-division. Slender shafts of fine purbeck marble stand out in bold relief from the subsidiary arcade of lancet arches behind. The whole conception makes a most effective counterpoint to the strong arches of the arcade below and of the clerestory above.

In the centre of the chancel, before the high altar, is the tomb of King John who, following his own request, was buried here in 1216, between the shrines of St. Oswald and St. Wulstan. The tomb has the oldest surviving royal effigy in England, and contains the remains of the first medieval king to be buried in this country. The choir is raised above the Norman crypt which was begun in 1084 and is generally regarded as one of the loveliest in England.

Wulstan of Worcester, the only Saxon bishop to retain his see

The Norman Crypt, Worcester Cathedral

after the Conquest, had deplored the demolition of the Saxon church of his predecessor St. Oswald, 'We poor wretches destroy the work of our forefathers that we may get praise for ourselves.' In 1092 he summoned a synod to meet in the crypt which he dedicated to St. Oswald. Before the ambulatory was blocked, to support the thrust of the choir above, the crypt was a forest of more than seventy, slender Norman pillars.

On the south side of the choir, in a bay adjoining the altar, is the sumptuous chantry chapel of Prince Arthur, the eldest son of Henry VII, who died of pneumonia at Ludlow Castle in 1502, only five months after his marriage to the Princess Catherine of Aragon. (See Walk 30). The chapel is a superb example of Tudor Gothic style, and has such a marked resemblance to Henry VII's chapel at Westminster Abbey as to suggest that the same masons were employed here. The delicate enclosing stone screens are divided into compartments by slender, paired buttresses faced with tiers of niched figures. About halfway up the screen a range of solid panels is embellished with familiar Tudor emblems − the rose, the portcullis, the falcon and fetterlock, the sheaf of arrows, and included here, the pomegranate of Aragon. The interior of the chapel is richly overlaid with panelling, and in niches in the reredos on the east wall, there are carved figures, alas today sadly mutilated. In the centre the granite tomb of the prince has the arms of England and France on the side panels.

The tower which was completed in 1374 is the earliest of the Perpendicular cathedral towers. Beautiful in design it is one of the best known and most loved landmarks in all England. At the moment of writing, this superb tower is in danger of collapse due to the serious decay of its supporting piers. The cathedral authorities are urgently appealing for funds to avert such a disaster. Please give generously when you have enjoyed your brief tour of the building.
3.   From the cathedral, walk along the Deansway to what was, until 1840, the Bishop's Palace. The 14th century basement still houses the kitchen of the old abbot's lodging. Today the building with its Georgian facade serves as a diocesan centre.
4.   At the top of Deansway stands another famous Worcester landmark − the Glover's Needle, the tower and 245 feet tall spire, all that remains of St. Andrew's church, retained to relieve an otherwise featureless skyline. This graceful monument, the work of Nathaniel Wilkinson, is in height second only to the spire of Salisbury cathedral.

5. Continue along Deansway, where, at the junction with Bridge Street, stands All Saints church, the work of the Worcester architect Thomas White, a gifted pupil of Sir Christopher Wren. Unfortunately much of White's pleasantly restrained classical temple was torn down in a barbaric restoration in 1888.

In the south aisle there is a memorial to Samuel Matthew who died in 1676. The smiling, rubicund, complacent face is surely the epitome of the successful, self-made city father of all ages.

6. From Deansway, turn right along Broad Street, and then left to reach Foregate Street and the Berkeley Hospital, which was built in 1672 in a most attractive Dutch style by Robert Berkeley, who had served as a diplomat at the Hague in the reign of Charles II. The Hospital stands in a neat, flagged courtyard with a small chapel at the far end. Ring the custodians' bell to gain admission to the chapel where there is a life-size, painted statue of the patron Robert Berkeley himself, complete with scarlet coat and fine Steenkirk collar.

The Guildhall, Worcester

7. From Foregate Street, retrace steps to the High Street to find Thomas White's splendid Guild Hall built between 1717 and 1724. The building stands on the site of the Hall of the Merchants' Guild founded in the 13th century, and which for hundreds of years was also the centre of the governors of the city, the local court of justice and the city jail.

Today the bright, brick building is decorated most vividly with stone dressing, while the imposing facade celebrates, possibly a touch too blatantly, the triumph of the Stuarts in 1660. The doorway and central bays are framed by huge Corinthian columns, and surmounted by an elaborately carved Hanoverian coat of arms. Above the entrance, the carved figure of Queen Anne, and the figures of Charles I and Charles II on either side of the doorway, were probably the work of the architect. On the parapet the five figures staring out over the street, represent Labour, Peace, Justice, Plenty and Chastisement. The inner hall originally accommodated the law courts and the fine upper room was used as a council chamber and assembly room.

The Guild Hall is open to the public:
Monday – Friday, 9.30 am – 4 pm.

8.   From the Guild Hall walk left along the High Street and turn right down St. Swithin's Lane to pass St. Swithin's church and reach King Charles' House at the corner of New Street and the Cornmarket. Prince Charles stayed here in 1651 and is said to have escaped from the rear of the house after the royalist defeat in the city. It was the town house of the Berkeley family who now occupy Spetchley Park.

9.   Quite close in New Street is Nash's House. John Nash set up glove making in Worcester in the 16th century, and also built the Nash and Wyatt Almshouses.

10.   From New Street continue in the same direction to reach Friar Street, and on the left, find Greyfriars, a superb late 15th century timber-framed house, which was the guest house of the friary. Magnificently restored it is now the property of the National Trust.

Greyfriars is open to the public: April to October
Wednesdays, Thursdays and Bank Holidays from 2 – 6 pm.

11.   Close to Greyfriars on the opposite side of the street is the Tudor House which has also survived from the 15th century, and which has been at various times in the past, an inn, a shop, a clinic and is now a most attractive museum. Tudor House is open: Monday to Saturday, from 10.30 am to 5 pm, but is closed all day on Thursday.

Across the street the Laslett Almshouses were erected in 1912 to improve the accommodation of the old prison.

12.   From Friar Street continue in the same direction to join

The Commandery

College Street then turn left to reach Sidbury, cross the canal bridge and find the Commandery which was founded as a hospital by St. Wulstan in 1085, and throughout the middle ages was governed by a preceptor as a commandery of the Knights Hospitallers.

The present building is late 15th century and has undergone a good deal of recent restoration. There is a fine timbered great hall with an eye-catching oriel window, which is adorned with elegant, glazed panels. In the upper room, which is reached by a sturdy Elizabethan staircase, are some murals which depict scenes from the Bible. During the Battle of Worcester in 1651, the building served as the main Royalist headquarters.

The Commandery is open to the public:
Monday – Saturday, 10.30 am – 5pm.
Sunday, 2 – 5 pm.

13. From the Commandery, cross the road and turn left along King Street to reach Severn Street and the Royal Worcester Porcelain Works, whose wares can rank with some of the world's best porcelain.

The manufacture of porcelain at Worcester was started by Dr. John Wall of Malvern Water fame (see Walk 22), who sought to revive the city's waning prosperity following the decline in the woollen cloth trade in the 18th century. He experimented and found a substitute for the china clay which was not found in Britain, and

173

in 1751 opened a factory where craftsmen copied Chinese and Japanese porcelain, and the popular wares of Meissen, Dresden and Sèvres. The factory was a success, gifted designers were attracted to Worcester and today examples of their work are on display in the Dyson Perrins museum which is near the factory.

The Worcester Porcelain Company
Open daily – 9 am – 5 pm.

Dyson Perrins Museum
April to September,
open Monday – Saturday,
10 am – 5 pm.

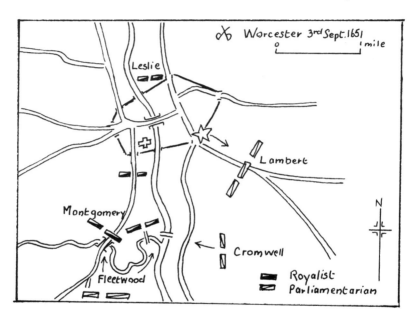

The Battle of Worcester, 3rd September, 1651.
Worcester changed hands several times in the opening phase of the Civil War, but was finally secured for the King at the end of 1642, and thereafter became one of the main Royalist strongholds and a base for operations across the Midlands and into the Welsh Marches. During the Royalist occupation the gates and walls of the city which had fallen into disrepair were strengthened, so that the city was able to repel all Parliamentary assaults until the defeat of the King's main army at Naseby in the summer of 1645.
By the Spring of 1646 all the surrounding region was in

Parliamentary hands, and in July of that year, after enduring siege and heavy artillery bombardment for two months, the Royalist garrison in Worcester surrendered to Parliamentary forces. In August 1651 a Royalist force commanded by Charles Stuart, and supported by a Scots army, marched on the city and on the 22nd of August the Parliamentary garrison withdrew and the Royalist army marched into Worcester unopposed.

The Prince set up his Court in the house in the Cornmarket which belonged to Rowland Berkeley, and immediately set about improving the city's defences in anticipation of the inevitable Parliamentary assault. Earthworks were thrown up beyond the walls, and a large star-shaped fort was built south-east of the city and linked to the walls by an earth rampart.

Cromwell's army appeared outside Worcester at the end of August and began preparations for the final attack. The main force took up a commanding position on Red Hill south of the city and began a steady bombardment. The west bank of the river was secured by the Parliamentarians and a force commanded by Colonel Fleetwood was stationed at Powick. Bridges of boats were built across the Teme and the Severn, to ensure contact between the two armies preparing for an assault on the city from two sides.

Early on the morning of the 3rd of September, which was fine and clear, the Prince climbed the tower of the cathedral and there held a council of war. To the south he could see all Cromwell's army drawn up on rising ground, and effectively covering the road to London. To the west he could see Fleetwood's army crossing the Teme and launching an attack on the Scots commanded by Montgomery. To assist Fleetwood's assault, which was being harassed by Royalist musketeers on the river bank, Cromwell ordered some of his force to build a bridge of boats across the Severn about a mile below the city.

Hoping to take advantage of this weakening of Cromwell's main army, Charles ordered a counter-attack. The Royalists marched out of the Sudbury gate and launched a frontal assault, and at first the enemy troops wavered and fell back. The Prince, it seems, distinguished himself by his dash and bravery, but his force was outnumbered and the Scots led by David Leslie failed to back up the Royalist attack. Leslie was a seasoned soldier; he understood the significance of the Prince's failure to attract any great support in England on the march south. More than 200 miles from Scotland, in a bitterly hostile country, Leslie wisely concluded that this was a battle well lost.

Cromwell meanwhile had quickly recognised that the Royalist assault had seriously over-extended their defending forces. He recalled the regiments opposing the Scots, recrossed the river with his main army, and drove the Royalists back into the city 'at push of pike.' By the end of the day 3000 Royalists lay dead in the streets of Worcester, 10,000 had been taken prisoner, many confined in the cathedral. Prince Charles having briefly returned to his lodgings in the Cornmarket, escaped by the back door as Colonel Corbett entered by the front. The 'crowning mercy' of Cromwell's victory at Worcester was to be the triumphant finale of his remarkable military career.

WALK 24
POWICK – CALLOW END – OLD HILLS – BRAYSWICK – POWICK.

O.S. Sheet No. 150 1:50,000 Worcester and the Malverns. Distance 5 miles. Grid Ref. 834515.

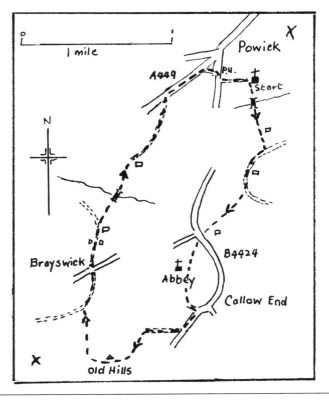

This is an easy ramble largely along firm tracks and over grassy pastures, with eye catching views throughout the walk.

There is a convenient car park at the church gates. Walk through the churchyard taking the grassy path to the right of the tower, which leads to a kissing gate opening into a small paddock. Cross the paddock, go through the double metal gates, go over the farm track and follow the path straight ahead, with an orchard on the right, and beyond, a splendid view of the Malvern Hills. Keep on the same heading to go through another metal gate, cross another tiny paddock, go under power lines and over a stream to walk along the well-marked path to the right of the sewage works.

Now cross an arable field keeping on the same heading to join a green lane coming from the left. Turn right along the lane to go past a white cottage when the way swings left and goes past a caravan site on the right. Continue straight ahead along an enclosed gully which soon emerges on to the B4424. Turn right and almost immediately, on the left side of the road, find a footpath sign near a kissing gate. Follow the enclosed path past St. Mary's House and the Abbey church to reach the B4424 again. The Benedictine abbey was moved here from Salford Priors in 1838 and the chapel attached to the abbey was built in 1871.

Turn right to walk through the pleasant village of Callow End. Go past the villlage hall and the school to find Bush Lane on the right. A few yards past Bush Lane and also on the right, turn along a surfaced track which leads past two small cottages and goes through a metal gate onto the rough pasture land of the Old Hills. Follow the main path up the slope to enjoy the wonderful view from the top of the Old Hills. Although barely 300 feet in height, the surrounding countryside is so flat that a remarkable vista unfolds from the top of the tiny ridge. The rugged Malverns so dominate the view to the west that they seem close enough to touch. To the south-east can be seen the rounded hump of Bredon Hill, to the north-east the Abberleys, and beyond, the Clent Hills and the Lickeys.

From the north end of the ridge descend to the left towards a white farm to meet a surfaced road. Turn right down a green lane which is badly churned up by tractors and could be rather muddy in wet weather. Reach a farm track and turn left for a short distance to reach Bush Lane. Turn right and then almost immediately left along a metalled track. Go past cottages to climb a lane which winds through a farmyard, and through a metal gate on the right walk down a pasture to reach another gate. The hospital buildings now stand out boldly on the slope to the left. Go under power lines and across a pasture to reach a metal gate opening onto a grassy bridge over a stream.

Climb the track towards an old, half-timbered farmhouse at the top of the slope. Through the gate, follow the metalled lane for about ¾ mile to reach the A449. Turn right to return to the church-yard and the car park. We found the fare at the 'Bluebell Inn' at Callow End highly recommendable.

Powick, once a small village of attractive Georgian villas has today become a dormitory of Worcester, and is largely a collection of nondescript bungalows built on the site of Powick Court. The ancient bridge, the lower part of which dates from the 15th century, was replaced by a bridge in the Gothic design in 1837.

The church in red sandstone which stands on a hill above the low-lying country has a nave and aisles which are Early English, and a 15th century tower which on its exterior bears the marks of musket fire from the Civil War. The interior of the church is noteworthy for two memorials, one to Sir Daniel Tyas, the mayor of Worcester, who was knighted for his support for the Royalist cause in 1651, and in the chapel on the north side, the striking monument to Mary Russell who died in 1786. It was sculpted by Thomas Scheemakers in beautiful white marble, and shows the graceful figure of a woman reclining on a sarcophagus which is adorned with musical instruments.

The Skirmish at Powick Bridge.

On the 27th May, 1642 Parliament declared war on Charles I, and during the ensuing summer months both sides were active securing and fortifying towns and strongholds throughout the country.

On the 22nd August the King raised the royal standard at Nottingham and began a march west to join Royalist forces which were being raised for him in South Wales. At that stage it was not clear where he was aiming for − Chester, Shrewsbury or Worcester, and the Earl of Essex commanding the main Parliamentary army at Northampton, was ordered to stay between the Royalist army and London, and also to cut off the King from his support in the west. Essex seems to have decided that the enemy's objective was Worcester and he marched west through Stratford and Pershore. One Parliamentary regiment was so enthusiastic about the prospect of ending Royalist resistance that they ran 'for two miles together crying "to Worcester, to Worcester" and entreated their officers to march all night to get at the enemy.'

Meanwhile the King had ordered a company of horse commanded by Colonel John Byron to Oxford to collect money which had been sent there by Royalist supporters, and to enlist as many recruits as possible. Having carried out these orders Colonel Byron marched on to Worcester, where he was joined by Prince Rupert, sent to protect him and his valuable baggage, which now included most of the Oxford Colleges' plate, with eight troops of horse and ten companies of dragoons. The Prince decided that the city's defences

179

were so decayed as to make Worcester untenable as a garrison, and prepared to withdraw to Shrewsbury where it had now been decided the main Royalist army would assemble for the march on the capital.

Essex had learned of Colonel Byron's arrival in Worcester, and sent Colonel Fiennes ahead with squadrons of cavalry to prevent the enemy from moving out of the city. Fiennes reached Worcester on the 22nd September, and made a demonstration outside the walls to advertise the presence of Parliamentary forces to the Royalists. He then crossed the river and took up a position at Powick where he could observe the advance of Essex, and at the same time cut off Colonel Byron, should he move out of the city.

The following day Prince Rupert with a number of his officers were reconnoitering the terrain south of the city when they became aware that troops of Parliamentary horse, part of Colonel John Brown's advance column, had crossed the river Teme at Powick, and were intending to cut them off. The Royalists were in an open field and to reach them, the Parliamentarians led by Colonel Edwin Sandys dashed headlong up a narrow lane between tall, quickset hedges. Here they were suddenly harassed by musket fire from Royalist dragoons, which checked them sufficiently long for Rupert to draw up his cavalry and deliver a full-blooded charge against the enemy as they emerged in disorder from the lane. The Parliamentarians fell back in utter confusion and as they galloped down on their comrades struggling up the lane, the order was given 'Wheel about', which the inexperienced troopers interpreted as 'Save yourselves'. They turned in chaotic disarray and so great was the terror of their flight that they fled nine miles to Pershore, where they met Essex's bodyguard of one hundred picked men and so discouraged them that they also turned and ran! Colonel Edwin Sandys, severely wounded, died during the night.

Although the affair at Powick Bridge was no more than a skirmish, its effect was out of all proportion to its military significance. A small party of experienced Royalist cavalry had routed a large force of inexperienced Parliamentarians. The following day the Earl of Essex issued a general order that his officers should without delay instruct their men 'in the necessary rudiments of war, that they may know to fall on with discretion and retreat with care.'

WALK 25
DROITWICH – COPCUT – SALWARPE – DROITWICH.

O.S. Sheet No. 150 1:50,000 Worcester and the Malverns. Distance 2½ miles.

First we suggest a short itinerary of Droitwich to discover what remains of interest in this ancient town, which was much prized by the Romans and which in recent times, has become engulfed by a sprawling mish-mash of motorway overspill and an unendearing clutter of modern housing estates.

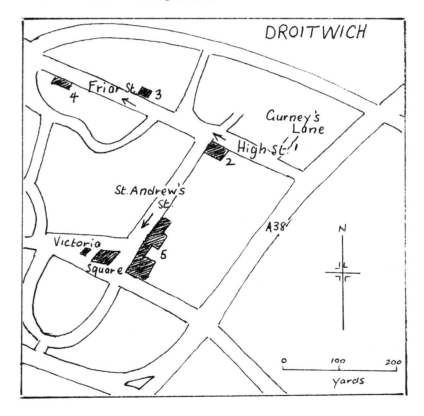

1.   From the car park behind the High Street go up Gurney's Lane, and on the left, find an interesting relic of the last salt works in

Droitwich, the base of the chimney of an old salt pan where the brine was evaporated, and part of the pumping mechanism which brought the brine to the surface. Continue into the High Street which dips down suddenly from the A38 so that some of the houses which lean drunkenly, show the effect of subsidence caused by the long term extraction of brine from beneath the town.

2. St. Andrew's Church at the west end of High Street had its steeple dismantled in 1928 when subsidence had made it dangerous. The bells were saved however and are neatly stored in the north aisle and in the chantry chapel.

The main part of the church dates from the 13th century, but there have been considerable additions and alterations in the 14th century and in more recent times. The chapel which is under the tower is dedicated to St. Richard de Wyche, a local boy who was to become Bishop of Winchester in the reign of Henry III, and according to legend, when the brine wells dried up, blessed them so that they flowed again.

We had the privilege of climbing up the steep, narrow stairway to the clock chamber, to witness the bi-weekly ritual of winding the splendid clock which was installed in the tower in 1910. Mute witnesses were half a dozen crudely carved heads which had once adorned the parapet of the dismantled upper storey. Up a short ladder a trap door gave access to the roof and superb views over Droitwich to the Malverns and the Clee Hills.

3. From St. Andrew's continue along Friar Street to inspect the 'Old Cock Inn' which was first granted a licence in 1712. A decorated window from the old St. Nicholas' church has been quite neatly incorporated into the frontage. The inn is said to have been used by Judge Jeffries as an assize court following the disastrous Monmouth Rebellion in 1685. The girning face on the wall near the doorway is said to be that of the detested judge.

4. At the east end of Friar Street and on the south side is Priory House, a sturdy timber-framed dwelling of the late Elizabethan period, which was given a chimney in the 18th century.

5. Return to St. Andrew's Street and on the south side, facing the spacious Victoria Square stands the Raven Hotel, which is on the site of the old manor of Wyche where St. Richard was born, the son of a yeoman farmer. The present building, much extended in recent times, dates from the 16th century.

About ¾ mile south along the A38 find the church of the Sacred Heart which was consecrated in 1932 and which is built in the style of a Roman basilica, with a simple nave and aisles, and a deep, semi-circular apse at the east end. The wide, uncluttered nave presents a most welcome change after so many churches over-burdened with obtrusive monuments often of little artistic merit.

The immediate impression is one of light, airy spaciousness, and of lively, joyous colour, albeit because of its newness perhaps a trifle strident. The walls of the nave are covered with mosaics designed by Gabriel Pippet and executed by Maurice Josey and Fred Oates. They are composed of millions of tesserae of coloured Venetian glass, and following the tradition of the early Christian churches, are intended to beautify the building and instruct worshippers in the tenets of the Faith. On the left side, the frieze below the clerestory windows displays scenes from the life of the Virgin Mary, and between the windows appear fourteen fathers of the church − St. Basil, St. Jerome, the Venerable Bede and so on. On the right side the frieze portrays scenes from the life of St. Richard of Wyche and between the windows appear fourteen prophets and patriarchs, − Moses, Abraham, Joshua, Daniel, etc. The spandrels are enhanced with medallions representing the twelve apostles.

Over the dome of the apse stands a huge figure of Christ with outstretched arms, and behind him a golden dome decorated with palm trees. Over the sanctuary arch is a portrayal of the Resurrection and on the west wall there is a truly splendid mosaic which represents the angelic host of archangels, angels, saints, princes and potentates according to the Scriptures.

The capitals of the piers of the nave arcade, also designed by Gabriel Pippet, are of particular interest. They follow the ancient Byzantine tradition and incorporate vine and acanthus foliage and are most effective in this colourful setting. A well-produced hand-book gives full details of all there is to be seen in the church, its chapels, the narthex and baptistry.

From the church of the Sacred Heart go along the A38 towards Worcester, turn right at the first island onto the A4133 and after about ½ mile find a small lay-by on the left, just before the bridge over the railway. Grid reference − 885620.

Close by on the left a path descends across rough pasture, with a plantation of saplings on the right, to a footbridge over a willow-lined stream. Over a stile, climb a grassy slope and continue with the hedgerow on the right. After about 60 yards find a stile on the right, go over and turn left over an arable field. On our walk the ripening grain was colourfully enlivened by patches of scarlet poppies. Climb another fence-stile in the corner and go alongside a short arable field to come out on the road at Copcut. Turn right to go past a delightful, timber-framed thatched cottage which has been extended with great success.

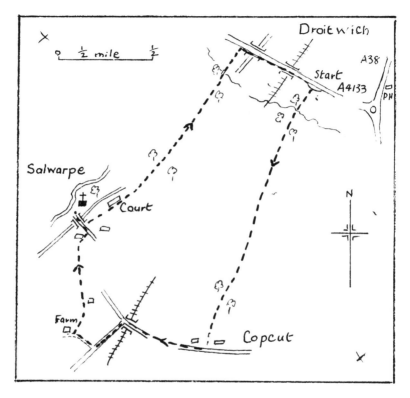

After about ½ mile go over the railway bridge and turn left along Ladywood Road for about 200 yards, and then turn right along a surfaced lane leading to Church Fields Farm. Just before the white, timber-framed farmhouse, turn right through a metal gate to cross a rough pasture and reach a gate on the left of a small cottage. Now go half-left across a meadow aiming for Salwarpe church ahead. Through a kissing gate beside a red brick house, go down an overgrown path to come out on Salwarpe bridge.

The church of St. Michael and all the Angels at Salwarpe has an idyllic setting on a woody slope above the river Salwarpe, and near the old mill. The church is approached through a lych gate and

Honeysuckle

across a neat churchyard with fine yew and thuya trees. It is a typical English village church, largely 14th century with a good deal of Victorian rebuilding, which was not entirely successful. Of special interest is the fine 17th century altar tomb in the south chantry chapel, and on the south wall of the chancel, the unusual and attractive miniature mural tablet with the kneeling figures of Thomas Talbot and his wife, and their son and daughters neatly arranged beneath them. The carving of all the figures is crisp and delicate. The reredos above the altar is modern and is a superb piece of sculptured alabaster representing the Last Supper, and was designed by James Powell.

From the church follow the direction of the footpath sign, go over the bridge on the left and cross the pasture with the haha and beyond, Salwarpe House on the left. Cross the drive to the house and go over two more stiles to cross a paddock, and then go along the edge of an arable field, keeping the hedge on the right. At the end of the field the path descends past a pond and goes over a footbridge. Climb the slope over rough ground with abundant gorse bushes and honeysuckle to come upon the A4133 again.

Turn right to go over the road bridge and then the railway bridge, to reach the lay-by and car park. The 'Red Lion' Inn near the island on the A38 is a homely pub offering very good refreshments.

1. Droitwich

About 200 million years ago the drying up of vast shallow lakes which had no outlet to the sea left behind immense deposits of salt which formed in layers up to 200 feet deep between the sandstone rock, and down to a depth of almost 200 feet. The Romans quickly recognised the value of these deposits and exploited the natural brine springs by setting up salt pits along the valley of the Salwarpe. They called the settlement Salinae and built roads to carry the salt to the legions stationed in all parts of the country.

The Saxons continued to use the salt pans and named the place Wic, probably after the Hwicce tribe who controlled the area, and to this name, in the reign of Edward III, the droit was added to show customary right of ownership and the grant of a royal licence to produce salt. By the 18th century the salt which hitherto had been extracted from natural springs, was pumped up through bore holes, a practice which eventually created huge caverns under the town and led to serious subsidence. As the market for salt grew, the Salwarpe canal was built in 1767 to connect the town via the river Severn with Birmingham and Bristol. The salt-grinding mills set up during this period have been converted to other uses.

The brine rising from the natural springs is eight times saltier than sea water, and in the 19th century some fashionable physicians recommended bathing in hot brine as helpful in the treatment of rheumatic diseases. Because of its favourable position in the Severn plain, sheltered by the Malvern Hills in the west, and by the Lickeys to the north, Droitwich was admirably sited for development as a health spa. That development was greatly assisted by the foresight and acumen of a local businessman, John Corbett, who had immense faith in the possibilties of the town as a spa at a time when taking the waters was becoming fashionable amongst Victorian well-to-do. Corbett built the Royal Brine Baths which were opened in 1836, and remodelled the old manor house which became the Raven Hotel, to accommodate visitors to the spa.

In the meantime Corbett had removed the main salt producing business to Stoke Prior to the north of the town. He lined the new brine pits with cast iron cylinders to check the inflow of fresh water which in times of flood or heavy rainfall had commonly caused the brine to rush to the surface and run to waste. Corbett's improved methods raised the annual output of salt from 26,000 to 700,000 tons.

In 1876 to gratify the whim of his French wife, John Corbett had built the Chateau Impney which stands near the A38 about ½ mile north of the town centre. He had acquired also seventy acres of park land which he now had professionally landscaped. An ornamental lake was designed with waterfalls, and crossed by artistic bridges. The park was improved with woodlands of a great variety of treees, while the sweep of the lawns and terraces was to be a miniature copy of those of the palace of Versailles, and similarly decorated with fountains and statues. Italian decorators were brought to work on the interior of the house which, it was believed, resembled a French chateau of the age of Francis I. A massive carved oak stair-case with marble pillars, connected the ground and upper floors. By day the light streamed in through stained glass windows, by night the pseudo-French palace was lit by acetylene gas. Today, the Chateau Impney, flamboyant almost to the point of vulgarity, seems curiously out of place in the Worcestershire countryside, but it is, we are told, a popular and successful hotel.

2. Salwarpe Court is a fine timber-framed house of the late 15th and early 16th centuries which replaced a moated grange of the 12th century. The house has been most carefully restored and is in an excellent state of preservation. The front has a deep bay window surmounted by a gable with elaborately carved barge boards. The doorway, with moulded posts and four-centred head has the original 15th century door − an excellent example of the fine quality of the joinery of that period.

The manor, originally held by the monastery at Coventry, was granted to Urso d'Abitot after the Conquest, and from him descended to the Beauchamp family. Richard Beauchamp, the 13th Earl of Warwick was born here on 28th January, 1381. (See Walk I). In 1487 the manor passed to Henry VII who settled it on Catherine of Aragon on her marriage to Prince Arthur in 1501. In 1546 it was sold to John Talbot, grandson of the Earl of Shrewsbury. Today the house is privately owned and not open to the public.

WALK 26
HANBURY HALL – PIPER'S HILL –
HANBURY – HANBURY HALL.

O.S. Sheet No. 150 1:50,000 Worcester and the Malverns. Start Point and Car Park National Trust Car Park Hanbury Hall Grid Ref. 947637.

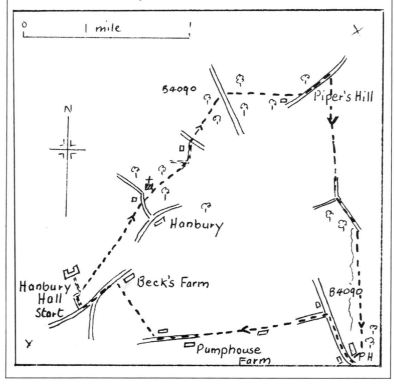

This is a pleasing ramble over countryside that was once ancient forest, and is now mainly pasture with a slight mixture of arable. There are still many fine trees dotted about the fields, and the hedges are not grubbed up. The going is level and the walk is made more interesting by the possibility of viewing Hanbury church and of course the fine Queen Anne mansion, once the home of the Vernons and now in the care of the National Trust.

From Hanbury Hall car park, facing away from the Hall go through a wooden gate and cross a grassy paddock to join a metalled road leading to the rear of the Hall. Turn left along the road and after about 200 yards, when it turns left, take the cart track which runs off to the right between rows of oak trees. Follow the track, go through a gate or over the stile and climb a pasture with Hanbury church on the hill in view. Go through a gate to the road and walk up past a house on the left, to the church, which is open during the hours of daylight and repays a thorough visit.

From the church go through a kissing gate in the far corner of the churchyard. The path drops down the hill past a pond on the right, crosses a meadow and goes through a gate opening onto a vehicle track. Keep on the track for about 100 yards, past a half-timbered house on the left and a tall oak, and then bear left to follow a grassy path which skirts the bottom edge of Piper's Wood. The path now joins another vehicle track, goes past another house on the left and a pool thick with bulrushes on the right, and climbs up through the trees to join the B4091.

Cross the road here, and slightly to the right find a path much overgrown with nettles which follows the left side of the wood. Where tracks meet go left through a field gate and walk down a concrete drive leading to a farm. Just before the farm go over a fence stile on the left and walk in a meadow with the wire fence on the right. Pass through two metal gates enclosing a sheep fold and go through an old orchard to a wooden gate admitting to a lane by a splendid thatched cottage with a pool in the garden.

In this lane go left and after ⅓ mile where it turns left, take a rough track which runs through trees on the right. This long track which lies below the ridge of Forest Hill is badly cut up by horses and tractors and makes the walking so much less enjoyable.

Where the track joins a lane, turn left and 100 yards further on where the lane divides, bear right. Pass a cottage and immediately go through a metal gate on the right. Cross a meadow to a pool, keep the hedge on the right and pass through a gap. Follow the edge of the field with the ditch and tall hedge on the left and keep your eye open for a bull. Go over a corner stile by a pond and continue alongside the brook to go over another stile. Now walk along the right-hand edge of the only arable field encountered during the day. Climb two corner stiles on the left and cross the brook, continuing now with the brook on the right. Continue across the wide meadow, following the hedge on the right to the field corner at the back of some houses.

The path loses itself here, so turn left behind the garage and bungalow to a field gate on the right. Beyond it is the B4090 and the 'Vernon Arms' is on the corner to right. We found the inn had good ale and offered a fair menu.

Continue the walk by going north along the B4091 and after ⅓ mile turn left along Pump House Lane. This is a quiet lane with wide grass verges and there are attractive half-timbered houses and pleasant cottages with tall chimneys to admire. After about ¾ mile pass a road junction on the left and Pump House Farm. A few yards further on, just beyond Grumbleground Cottage and almost opposite Nicholas Green, go through a gate and walk half right across rough pasture to find a corner stile. Continue on the same heading with Beck's Farm now clearly in view on the right. Go to the left of the farm and find a field gate which opens on to the road. Turn left and walk along the road to find the signposted entrance to Hanbury Hall car park.

Hanbury, variously spelled Heanburg, Heanberi, or Hambir in medieval times, is a hilly parish bisected by the Droitwich-Alcester road. Where the latter passes the 'Vernon Arms' on the left, a roadside inn whose sign depicts the family crest and motto 'Ver non semper viret' (Spring is not always green), a branch road leads up towards the church on a dominant knoll. Habington in the 17th century describes 'Hambury' as a 'stately seat meete for a Kinge's Pallace', and writes 'the church, invironed with highe and mighty trees and able to terrifye a far-off ignorant enimy with a deceitful showe of an invincible castell may rightly be called the Lanthorne of our County'. So it must have seemed then, set on its hill amid the vast Forest of Feckenham in the days before the timber had been consumed by the demands of the Droitwich salt industry and the emerging iron works of the Black Country, and still today it commands a wide view over the Worcestershire plain towards Malvern and the Lickeys.

The hill may well have been a fort in pre-Saxon times and later a monastery preceded the present church whose original dedication was to St. John the Baptist, but which was altered in 1553 in deference to Mary Tudor to Our Lady the Virgin. It is constructed in local sandstone, the south arcade dating from the early 13th century. The north aisle was added in the 14th and the tower, formerly known as 'The Hanbury Haycock', was rebuilt and embellished in 1795. The chancel was restored by the Victorian architect George Edmund Street who also added the Vernon chapel which contains the family monuments. The church has reminders of many changes through the centuries, with heavy buttresses on the south wall and even more massive supports on the north side. An old mass dial is scratched on one of these. Two small circular windows in the porch give fine views and illustrate the impressive situation of the building.

The history of the family who came to live here is written on their monuments in the chapel. The first Lord of Vernon in Normandy was ennobled by the Conqueror and the senior branch had their seat at Haddon Hall in Derbyshire, from where the Lady Dorothy Vernon was romantically supposed to have eloped in 1563 with her lover John Manners, thus uniting the Vernons with the Earls of Rutland at Belvoir. The Hanbury Vernons however originated from Wheatcroft in Cheshire and Richard Vernon was Rector of Hanbury for 47 years till his death in 1627. His son Edward bought the manor from the Leighton family, and the estate passed through two more generations till Thomas Vernon succeeded to it in 1678.

He was a successful barrister in the Court of Chancery who had amassed a considerable fortune and represented Worcester as a Whig till his death in 1721. He used this wealth to create the park and house of red brick with stone dressings supposedly designed by William Rudhall of Henley-in-Arden, though William Talman of Chatsworth fame and Robert Hook who planned Ragley Hall have also been given the honour.

Built in the reign of Queen Anne, it has all the marks of the post-Restoration style of domestic architrave made popular by Sir Christopher Wren and Sir Roger Pratt. The keynotes are rational-

Hanbury Hall

ism, geometric order and domestic comfort. It consists basically of a central block with two wings projecting front and back. The central hall is flanked with half columns and the window above is richly decorated. Above the architecture is a line of dormer windows surmounted by a cupola, clock and weather vane. Possibly the most striking feature of the exterior is the elegance and abundance of windows which make the interior so light and airy.

There are a number of family portraits of the Vernons in what was once the Oak Room, and integral to the house are the Thornhill paintings on the ceiling of the Long Room, and dominating the walls and ceiling of the staircase. They depict scenes from the life of Achilles. This extravagant, exuberant style of Italian baroque art was introduced into England by Antonio Verrio and had become fashionable with wealthy house builders by the end of the 17th century. The two leading exponents of this grandiose art form were Louis Laguerre and Sir James Thornhill who had worked at St. Paul's. He had established his reputation by works at Chatsworth and Greenwich Hospital, but it was probably his paintings for Thomas Foley, Vernon's neighbour at Stoke Edith, now destoyed by fire, which decided Thomas to employ Thornhill at Hanbury.

There are political overtones in the portrayal among the paintings of Dr. Sachaverel, a high church Tory, who preached against the Whig prosecution of Marlborough's wars with the French. The unfortunate doctor, indicated by the God Mercury, is about to be pursued by the Furies for his lack of patriotism. In fact, he was brought to trial by the Whigs who thereby lost the sympathy of Queen Anne and the general populace, and began to decline in political importance from this time.

The house contains so much of beauty and elegance, but the central panel of the chimney piece in a small study on the west side has historic implications. It shows the Prince of Wales' feathers above the thistle, rose, fleur de lys and Worcestershire pears. The panel was brought from Ticknell House, Bewdley, the residence chosen by James I for his eldest son Henry who became the first Prince of Wales entitled to wear the thistle in his insignia.

Thomas Vernon died childless and the house went to his cousin, Bowater Vernon, a man described as 'of weak mind and giddy head' whose vanity and extravagance squandered much of the family fortune. His monument, by Roubilliac, is in the chapel. His son however was described by the same authority as a 'man of great parts' and restored the situation, though he died prematurely in

1771. His widow secured an advantageous marriage for her young daughter Emma with Henry Cecil of the great Burghley family of Stamford, but he turned out to be spoiled, selfish and wasteful. The marriage failed, and Emma, neglected, fell in love with the local curate, the penniless and consumptive William Sneyd. They eloped, and after living at Dawlish for a while, the couple went to Lisbon for the sake of William's health. He died there in 1791 and Emma returned to marry Sneyd's friend John Phillips in 1795. When she died at Hanbury in 1828 she was by her own wish buried in a simple grave still to be seen in the churchyard, rather than in the family vault, and the estates passed to her cousin Thomas Shrawley Vernon.

Meanwhile, Henry Cecil, unable to face the sneers of his friends and neighbours and the demands of his creditors, had disappeared from Hanbury and taken lodgings with a farmer in the remote Shropshire village of Great Bolas, assuming the unlikely alias of 'John Jones'. Farmer Hoggins had a pretty 15 year old daughter Sally. The story now unfolds like a Victorian melodrama. 'John Jones' seduced pretty Sally Hoggins and was forced by Farmer Hoggins into a shotgun wedding. A divorce decree from Emma was granted him, and two years later, in 1793, on the death of his uncle, Henry Cecil, now Lord Exeter, took his new wife Sally to Burghley House where it seems she was readily accepted and became known as the 'Cottage Countess'.

For the next century or so, life proceeded calmly at Hanbury, and finally Sir George, second baronet, bequeathed the house and park to the National Trust in 1953, though Lady Vernon still resided there till her death in 1962. Although little of the furniture belonged originally to the house, it has been well chosen so that the interior conveys a fair image of a wealthy gentleman's country home in the 18th century.

The Hall is open to the public from May to September Wednesday — Sunday 2 – 6 pm.

WALK 27
GREAT WITLEY – ABBERLEY –
WALSGROVE AND WOODBURY HILLS
– GREAT WITLEY.

O.S. Sheet No. 138 1:50,000 Kidderminster and Wyre Forest. Distances (full walk) am. 1½ miles, pm. 5½ approx. Start point in free car park opposite Great Witley village hall on A443. Grid Ref. 759657.

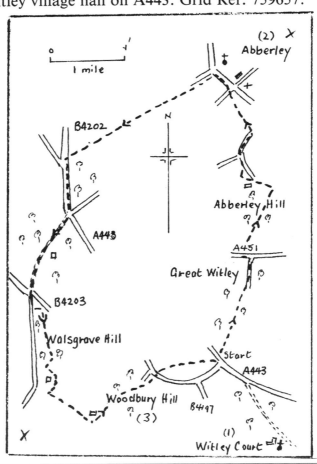

This walk in the delightful countryside of the wooded hills enclosing Abberley and Great Witley comes as a pleasant surprise to those used to rambling on the flat Midlands plain. It provides extensive views towards the Clees, the Malvern hills and over the Teme valley and the going is varied, arduous in places, with plenty of ascent and descent especially over Woodbury Hill, site of an Iron Age fort and later the base for Owen Glendower on one of his excursions into England. The tracks here are difficult to pick up when the bracken is high, but it is a rewarding walk for the purist, whilst for those wishing to combine pleasant exercise with a visit to the ruins of Witley Court and the exquisite baroque church there, we recommend a shortened version as indicated in the text. Correct attire and footwear is essential at all times, especially in winter.

Having parked in the free car park, look for a stepstile halfway down the right-hand hedge as you stand with your back to the road. Over this, a path crosses the arable field diagonally left to a metal gate in the left-hand corner which gives access to a road. Go left up to the junction with the A451 Stourport road, and left again along it to a bridle way sign on the right at the end of the houses indicating Shavers End. Now the climb up Abberley Hill begins and the enclosed path rises steadily to a crossing track at some orchards, goes straight over it, and enters the wood through a hunting gate. It then veers left into an open space affording a glimpse of Woodbury Hill opposite, climbs steeply and veers right through bracken to the top.

Dogs Mercury

Go left and start the descent through the trees, past a fork in the path and straight on down alongside banks of dog mercury to a stile at the edge of the wood, to emerge into a field with a white cottage on the left. Cross to the right-hand corner where a stile in the wire fence admits to the drive. Just before the iron gate on the left is a white gate leading into another field. Cross this half right to a gateway in the corner, enjoying the views of the wooded hills. A green footpath sign points back to Great Witley.

Go left up the lane between houses and pass to the right of Rose Cottage and continue down the hill to the junction. Here, turn left and walk up the village street past the Forge, now a garage. The 'Manor Arms' is ahead opposite the ancient church of St. Michael. We found the welcome here warm and the food and ale excellent. We had covered approximately 1½ miles as the crow flies, but there had been plenty of ascent and descent.

After refreshment turn right on leaving the inn, going west over the junction and leaving a tall handsome house on the left. Over the field to the right rises the spire of Abberley's Victorian church. There is a kissing gate on the same side, then on the left a footpath sign for Abberley Common. Leave the road and follow the hedge on the left to a gate, then on the same heading, walk with an iron fence on the right and a wood on the left. At an iron gate ahead turn left up the B4202, going uphill past Oak Lodge with the astonishing Abberley Clock Tower in view. Continue to the A443 Worcester-Tenbury road, turn left up it for a few yards, cross, and take the bridleway on the right for Stanford Road. This skirts the grounds of Abberley Hall, now a school, passing the clock tower amid the trees, and overlooking on the right a herd of grazing red deer obviously kept for commercial reasons.

The track emerges into the school grounds where a close-up of the tower is possible before proceeding straight on under the trees with the school playing fields on the left. The drive leads down to the lodge and main gates of wrought iron. It is possible, either here or at the beginning of the drive, to cut the walk short and return to Great Witley by the B4203 and A451, passing before the Hundred House Hotel on the way, but for the hardened walker the way now goes up the B4203 for a short distance and turns right up a lane at a white house called the Old Turnpike. Immediately on the left a stile admits to a field, and the path begins to wind up the slope of Walsgrove Hill, 800 feet high, from whose grassy summit there are magnificent views to the Clees and over the Teme valley, as well as

Lady's Bedstraw

towards the Clock Tower and the school grounds. The countryside is a patchwork of hedges, fields and woods, as yet unspoiled by the plough.

Follow the ridge in the same direction, south, passing over a stile and along the hedgerow. It is superb walking over springy turf which supports mallow, bedstraw and other plants. The trees are mainly oak and hawthorn. A third stile by an electricity pole leads into a wood. The path goes through it, passing a stile on the left, and begins to descend to the right, becoming difficult and slippery. Eventually after some tricky patches it arrives at a stile at the bottom. Over this it continues up through a conifer belt, passing over two stiles and climbing up to a Worcestershire Way sign, yellow on a white background, pointing right.

Go right, passing a white house on the left, to an iron gate, then along the lane past the houses to another yellow sign, walking down the grassy lane to a stile. The way wends through a copse, goes right, then left and drops through a wood to a lane. Turn left along this and continue round the bend, passing on the right the premises of Vinexports Ltd, a handsome house once called Woodbury old Farm. About 150 yards beyond, look for a walkers' sign on the left, high up in the hedge, and climb up the bank to the field. Now go slightly left up the field, heading for a hedge gap. These are the lower slopes of Woodbury Hill. Pass through the gap and continue up the next field through another gap. In the third field follow the left-hand edge to corner and enter the wood. There are some substantial farm buildings and a modern house in the right-hand corner. Turn left along a path to an iron gate. Just before it on the right, an obscure path overgrown with bracken and willow-herb begins the steep ascent. Fallen fence posts hidden in the undergrowth are a hazard here. The path eventually passes underneath two huge chestnut trees, turns right under others, and passes through bracken and bramble to join another marked path leading left to the top.

Rosemary Willow-herb

Here, after the difficulties of the climb there are wide clear rides. Take the one leading straight ahead through the wood, which winds down to a lane at the bottom. Turn right and continue down to a lane junction. Now go left up the road which leads to the B4203 and return to Great Witley by the A443 after a long and interesting, if sometimes difficult, route.

1. Witley Court and Church. The gaunt ruins of this once great centre of Edwardian fashion and affluence set in the gentle Abberley Hills cannot fail to impress, as they suddenly appear above the hedges of the A443. As is fitting, they are approached by a narrow rutted driveway flanked by the shrubs, trees and lake of a park almost as ruinous as the stark walls of the house itself which have now been stabilised and made relatively safe by English Heritage. As the visitor roams through the great rooms and strolls in the grounds once so carefully tended and adorned with fountains and terraces, he may well ponder on the vagaries of chance which one night in 1937 in the absence of the owner, caused fire to rage through the palatial apartments and reduced one wing to smoking ruin. Vandalism and neglect completed the destruction but the beautiful baroque church on which so much loving care and expense had been lavished, was spared, and stands today in all its magnificence in the care of Mr. Bill Pardoe, historian and voluntary custodian.

It could be said that this was a fitting end to a house which belonged essentially to an age of privilege and inequality, when life for the rich was never better and for the poor hardly ever worse. The luxury of the late Victorian and Edwardian eras and the values epitomised in country house society were brought to an end by the Great War of 14–18, and in a sense there was no more use for a building totally dedicated to those times; but the splendour of the church is ageless and the tragedy of the fire for the domestic building is mitigated by the miraculous survival of the ecclesiastical one.

The early history of the house is closely associated with the rise to fortune of the Foley family, one of whom, Thomas, had established at Stourbridge the beginnings of the iron industry in the County. His son, also Thomas, bought the Witley estate in 1655 and with the increasing wealth derived from the expanding iron works the first Thomas' grandson, Lord Foley, one of the many Tory peers created in 1712 to swamp the Whig majority in the Lords, rebuilt the Jacobean house and vastly improved the estates which in 1838 passed into the hands of the Earl of Dudley. Now began a period of unparalleled magnificence as Dudley lavished wealth on the house and garden where James and William Forsyth, local sculptors from Worcester, constructed the massive fountain of Perseus and Andromeda which still stands forlornly before the ruins. It is said that with its huge jet it was one of the biggest sculptures in Europe, and looking at it now one can picture the young gilded scions of the aristocracy who flocked to the house, disporting themselves in its waters.

The Dudleys strove to create here a fashionable centre for the high society of the times and spared no expense or luxury in doing so. Shooting parties, balls, country house receptions, the entertainment

199

of Royalty, especially Edward VII in this secluded spot, all combined to make the place the wonder of the Midlands and a source of a great deal of local gossip. Queen Adelaide, widow of William IV, resided here briefly. The wealth for all this came from the smoking industries of the Black Country where life was far different for the workers. Later the place passed into the ownership of Sir Herbert Smith, a Kidderminster businessman whose fortunes, derived from the carpet and blanket industries, were as great as those of the Dudleys, and though with the coming of the Great War the elegant life-style of the Edwardians was swept away, the house continued to be kept up in the way it was formerly, until one night in 1937 fire finally reduced it to the shell it now is.

The Foleys however seem to have possessed the instinctive style of the 18th century in addition to the wealth that enabled them to indulge it in the embellishment of the newly-built church of St. Michael and All Angels. Some may consider it a trifle florid for sober English tastes, and indeed it comes initially as a visual shock to see its balustrades and gilded dome in such a pastoral setting. Not for nothing though has it been called the finest Baroque church in the country, for the second Lord Foley was able to assemble here in his new-built chapel some of the best features from Canons, the recently-demolished palace of his friend the first Duke of Chandos, at Edgeware. The latter had amassed a colossal fortune as Paymaster General to Marlborough, but after his death his son sold the property, and Foley bought many of its fittings for his church, which stands today beside the derelict, roofless ruin of Witley Court.

It is a most unusual, exciting excursion into the rococo style of interior decoration more familiar in Bavaria. The magnificent glass windows designed by Sebastiano Ricci were painted by Joshua Price of York in 1719. The great ceiling painting of the Ascension and the smaller ones of the Nativity and the Descent, the work of Antonio Belluci, were also from Canons and have been skilfully incorporated into the overall design of the chapel by James Gibbs. The stucco effect on the ceiling was achieved by the use of the new invention of papier mâché, and on all sides we see the work of the best craftsmen. The wall panels gleam with white and gold, and not an inch is left unadorned.

The furnishings too are superb, the pulpit is elaborately carved with flowers and scenes from Our Lord's ministry, and the marble font resting on kneeling angels is the work of James Forsyth. The

Victorian pews have carved poppyheads, and the mosaic reredos in the sanctuary represents the lilies of the field. Above it, is Price's Resurrection window. The organ case from Canons once belonged to the instrument played by Handel who was resident musician there. It should perhaps come as no surprise to the visitor dazzled by all this splendour to find the towering monument by Rysbrack to the first Lord Foley presiding over it all with his family scuplted in the fashion of the times, an indulgence for which he may be forgiven since he has left us such a study in visual delight.

2.   Abberley. The astonishing Gothic clock tower with neat oriel window which dominates the approach from all sides and is visible all over the County was built between 1883 and 1885 by J.P. Aubyn for Squire John Jones, whose money was made in Lancashire cotton. He wished, not for a monument, but for a place from which he could look down on his aristocratic neighbour the Earl of Dudley at Witley Court. The tower 161 feet high, holds a set of 20 bells which can provide 42 tunes.

Abberley Hall was rebuilt after a fire in 1842 and was further enlarged by Squire Jones in 1880–8. Today it is in use as a private school.

There are two churches in the village – St. Michael's is Norman, ivy-clad, and was largely ruinous, and St. Mary's was built in 1852 of red brick after another fire. St. Michael's was built by the de Todenai family, Lords of the Manor, on Saxon foundations, and after many changes over the centuries fell into ruin, perhaps because the stone was too soft and the additions had made the building top-heavy. In 1850 the new church of St. Mary's became the centre of worship for the village, but in 1963 St. Michael's was stabilised by a group of volunteers who demolished the unsafe walls and restored the chapel. The result is a delightful little building in a peaceful setting, enhanced by the timber-framed modernised rectory still occupied by the incumbent. The treasures of St. Michael's include the 14th century silver spoons found in the wall at the time of the 1963 work, now in the British Museum, and the great cracked monastery bell brought here by one John Blaymire from the north, when he was made Rector by Henry VIII after the dissolution.

The village inn, the 'Manor Arms' displays the shields of the former owners of the manor, ranging from the de Todenais through such as the Beauchamps, the Watsons, the Bromleys, and the Jones.

3.   Woodbury Hill. Henry Stafford, Duke of Buckingham, who

had played a leading role in securing the throne for Richard III,

> *'Give me your hand. Thus high by thy advice*
> *And thy assistance, is King Richard seated.'*
>> *(King Richard III, Act IV sc.ii)*

in 1483 turned against the King when Richard declared that the sons of his brother Edward IV were illegitimate.

Raising the standard at Brecon, Buckingham moved east with a Welsh army to confront Richard who was reported to be at Coventry. On the Malvern Hills he was joined by the forces of Dorset and Salisbury, and now, several thousands strong the 'Army of Edward V' marched east in appalling weather, aiming to cross the Severn at Upton. Due to the incessant rain the flood-waters had risen so high that the bridge was impassable, and indeed the whole of the lower Severn valley was a vast lake.

Buckingham turned north hoping to cross the river at Worcester but the crossing there was also impassable and the army was compelled to seek higher ground until the floods subsided. Exhausted and hungry the soldiers encamped on Woodbury Hill in makeshift tents, and day after day were lashed by heavy rain. The men deserted in hundreds during the night and finally Buckingham's main ally withdrew his forces.

> *'The news I have to tell your Majesty*
> *Is, that by sudden floods and fall of waters,*
> *Buckingham's army is dispers'd and scatter'd:'*
> *And himself wanders away alone, no man knows whither.'*
>> *(King Richard III, Act IV, sc.iv)*

Buckingham fled north to be taken at Shrewsbury and brought to Salisbury for execution. Unfortunately, his luckless rebellion almost certainly sealed the fate of the young sons of Edward IV.

WALK 28
BEWDLEY – BUTTON OAK –
BEWDLEY.

O.S. Sheet No. 138 1:50,000 Kidderminster and Wyre Forest. Distances a.m. 4 miles, p.m. 4 approx. Car park in Bewdley just north of St. Anne's church. Grid Ref. 785754.

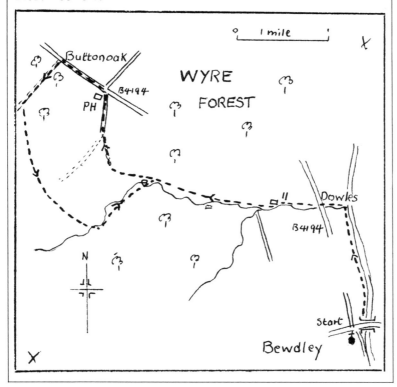

This walk in the Wyre Forest provides a welcome change of scene. The whole day is spent amid the varied trees of this extensive ancient woodland. We pass alongside Dowles Brook, through glades of beech, oak, beech and conifer. The forest paths are well-defined but the morning route can be slightly tricky unless the instructions are closely adhered to. The going is not arduous but can be muddy.

Deer

With any luck, the walker will catch a glimpse of deer leaping across the path or grazing in the glades, and one of the features of the day is the number and size of the anthills constructed by wood ants at the side of the track from the conifer needles.

Bewdley itself is a charming and historic town with many interesting buildings, all worth seeing. A labelled sketch map is supplied for a town tour, and a choice of two walks is available according to the time and energy of the walker.

For the longer route, start from Telford's bridge and walk north along the quayside past the Mug House Inn which was the favourite rendezvous of the bow-hauliers who man-handled the river boats or trows upstream, in the days when Bewdley's prosperity depended on the busy river traffic. Walk alongside the Severn for about ½ mile passing a complex of modern bungalows and a caravan site on the left and clumps of comfrey on the river bank. Then cross the Dowles Brook by a railed bridge at a point where the piles of the old railway bridge stand up gauntly in the river. Turn left along a dirt track to reach the B4194. Go right for about 100 yards, then turn left along an enclosed footpath which soon passes Dowles Manor on the right, a small timber-framed Elizabethan house almost completely destroyed by fire a few years ago and now undergoing a course of restoration.

At a metalled road, bear right and at the next junction take the right fork to follow the Dowles Brook upstream, past a neat cottage on a corner. This leads to Knowles Mill, which ceased production about 80 years ago when a horse and cart ran into the stream and shattered the mill wheel. Today the fine old corn mill has been transformed into a most attractive dwelling.

Carry on along the path which rises and becomes stone-paved, with the brook on the left to reach Cooper's Mill, now newly refurbished as a Youth Training Centre. There are some fine upstanding young trees hereabouts. A little way beyond the Centre take the right fork and climb away from the brook, ignoring a minor track on the right about a hundred yards further on, and continue steadily upward through the forest. When the path divides, take the right fork which doubles sharply back to the right, soon afterwards to emerge in a clearing, and at a track junction where sawn timber is stacked, keep right along a well-defined track.

This leads to a green gate with a stile alongside. Cross it and follow a hedged path which soon passes houses and leads to the B4194. Turn left to the 'Button Oak' Inn where we found a welcoming landlady, good ale, and satisfying food.

From the inn continue left, west along the B4194 for about ⅓ mile and re-enter the forest by a signposted Forestry Commission bridle path next to a house on the left. About half a mile from the road turn left along a track signposted 'Bridle Path' and then go right down a broad ride until a marker post is reached on the left, indicating a minor track. Follow this and taking the first right fork descend to a track junction and turn left to come to a T junction.

Here, go right, and right again at the next junction, following the bridle path signs, and right again to walk along a broad path at another T junction. The way now dips quite steeply and goes left to bridge a stream, then climbs and bends right. At a crossways with a narrow track turn left to descend and then climb, before following the bridle path sign which is across a broad track. The path now drops down to the Dowles Brook. Turn left and, ignoring the tempting footbridge, continue on the north bank alongside the stream for ½ mile before going right to cross a wooden vehicle bridge at a wide clearing and track junction with a large pool on the left. Continue following the brook to ford a tributary and a little way ahead now on the south bank leave the main track where it goes right. A little way further along the path a railed footbridge leads leftwards to the north bank. About a hundred yards on is the Youth Training Centre and the path back to Bewdley traversed on the outward journey.

WALK 29
BEWDLEY — RIBBERSFORD — BEWDLEY.

O.S. Sheet No. 138 1:50,000 Distance 2½ miles. Grid Ref. 786753.

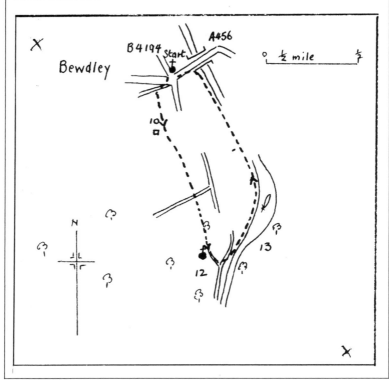

The shorter route, also described in 'Six Counties' Walks', is 2½ miles in length and suitable for a family afternoon stroll. It starts from Dog Lane, using the same car park, and goes past the 'Horn and Trumpet' inn, then turns left past the church to go up Park Lane for about 100 yards. Then it goes up the path on the left behind the almshouses and along the brick track to a kissing gate, where it passes alongside a corrugated fence on the left. The elevated site of Tickenhill Manor is on the right.

The rambler here goes through another gate past some chestnut

Comfrey

fencing, passing a large pond on the right as the way descends. Some large oaks flank the route before it rises under lime trees, to come to a road, across which it leads on the left of an arable field down to a rough track. The church of St. Leonard is on the right at the bottom of the track opposite a group of large barns.

Here, turn left down a lane with horse chestnuts to the B4194. Ribbesford House with its twin cupolas is on the right. Go left along the road to the corner where it turns sharp left, to find a gap on the right leading to the river bank. Walk to the left through clumps of comfrey and balsam with the river, wide and smooth, on the right. It is easy and pleasant going, and soon Blackstone Rock appears on the opposite bank, then the sports ground on the left comes into sight, with the quayside and bridge soon after.

Bewdley, an elegant, attractive Georgian town, was originally Wribbenhall in Saxon times, and was renamed Beau Lieu when the manor and estate were granted by the Conqueror to Roger de Mortimer, the powerful Marcher baron whose task was to keep the peace along the Welsh border. The Mortimers came to rule, in time, most of the border lands based on Wigmore and Ludlow castles, and a Welsh gate stood in Bewdley until 1822.

John Leland visited the town in 1540 and described it as 'set on the syd of an hill so coningly that a man cannot wishe to set a towne better. It riseth from the Severne bank so that a man standing on the hill trans pontem by este may descrive every house in the towne, and at the rysinge of the sonne the whole towne gliterithe, being all of new buyldinge, as it were of gold.' (Itinerary 1535–43).

From earliest times there were industries here – tanneries, cap making, and the fashioning of household articles from horn, but the wide stone-built quays on either bank of the river are reminders of the most prosperous days of Bewdley from the 16th to the late 18th century, as a busy inland port and trading centre.

The roads were often seas of mud in winter, or deserts of sand in summer, permitting at best only the passage of lightly-loaded pack-horses, or cumbrous, slow-moving carts. From the early Middle Ages until the 19th century, rivers were used as the main arteries of inland transport. Bristol, the main port of the south-west, was also, after London, the country's largest sea port, and from it the Severn penetrated right into the interior of the country, carrying more commercial traffic than any other English river, much of it destined for onward distribution from Bewdley, the furthest navigable point.

In the 18th century, upstream came wines, spices, tea, sugar, cotton and even slaves from the Caribbean. From Bewdley, Bridgnorth, Worcester and Gloucester were shipped local products – cloth, wool, timber, cheese and metal goods, keeping the quays busy and bringing great wealth to the merchants. This wealth is reflected in the fine Georgian houses lining the quayside, and scattered through the town.

The flat-bottomed river boats or trows which carried these goods were built in Bewdley and the local trow-masters sought to secure all the river traffic of the port for themselves by fair means or foul. A 16th century petition from the citizens of Gloucester and Bristol complains that 'certain persons of Bewdley having great boats called trowes, had confederated themselves together for their singular profit, and would let no other pass through the said port with their goods and chattels except they hire the said boats for the carriage of the said goods and that on the eve of St. Michael last past, they had seised upon a great dray or flote going to Gloucester, such as complainants had used to carry their timber and fuel, and made the masters of it cut it in pieces, the said flote on the said water, or otherwise they would cut off their heads'.

As navigation became more difficult north of Bewdley, cargoes were transferred to the smaller, flat-bottomed trows which were dragged upstream by labourers known as bow-hauliers, who were clearly a rough lawless breed. When in 1761 Parliament passed an act which permitted horses to be used to pull river boats, it met with the most violent opposition from the bow-hauliers, whose headquarters were the Mug House on Coles quay, where traditionally they met, were hired to haul boats, and sealed their contracts with a mug of ale.

In the 1700s it was proposed that James Brindley should be engaged to plan and build a canal linking the Severn and the Trent-Mersey canal near Bewdley. Stubbornly the proud corporation refused to have anything to do with the 'stinking ditch' and as a result Brindley constructed the Staffordshire — Worcestershire canal to join the Severn at Lower Mitton, which rapidly developed into the inland port of Stourport, and Bewdley's trade dwindled accordingly.

The town has a superb position on the right bank of the Severn, where the river runs between steep banks through what remains of the Wyre Forest to the north and goes swiftly across red sandstone rocks to the south.

WALK 30
A WALK AROUND BEWDLEY

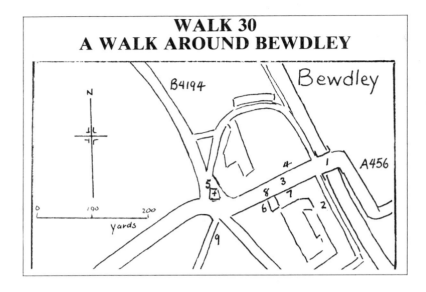

1. *The town is approached across Thomas Telford's graceful 3-arched bridge with its dainty, vase-shaped stone balusters. The toll house which was built on the left bank and planned by Telford as an integral part of the design had to be removed to assist the modern traffic flow.*
2. *Immediately on the left across the bridge is a row of fine houses and warehouses standing behind a wide sandstone quay, built to accommodate ocean-going vessels in the past. The 17th, 18th and 19th century houses are all worthy of note. River House which dates from the late 17th century has a fine wooden cornice and a central pedimented first floor window which opens onto a balcony. The shell-hooded doorway is most impressive.*
3. *Load Street has on the north side the 'George Hotel', an old timber-framed building, a posting house which happily has retained its carriage way and inside has an oak overmantel which came from Ribbesford House.*
4. *No. 71 has attractive flanking Palladian windows and white voussoirs which stand out most effectively against the plum-coloured brickwork.*
5. *The fine, classically simple St. Anne's church was built in the 18th century to replace an ancient wooden structure. Its graceful, uncluttered interior has Venetian windows and Doric columns, with*

the town's coat of arms − an anchor over a rose and a sword enclosed in a fetterlock − prominently displaying the motto 'Pro Deo, Rege, Grege − For God, the King, and the People'.

6.   The Museum on the site of the old shambles reflects aspects of the town's former prosperity − local crafts such as rope making, smithing, brass-founding and coopering are displayed in the arcades along the cobbled streets, at the end of which are two cells which were used for the detention of malefactors. There is also a brass foundry which turns out artefacts on a commercial basis, and a showcase containing mementoes of Bewdley's most famous son, Stanley Baldwin, who was Prime Minister in the 20s and 30s.

7.   The Post Office with three gables and overhangs dates from 1638 and has an eye-catching 18th century entrance of serpentine contour.

8.   The Town Hall from the early 19th century is handsome and quite dignified with Doric pilasters and tastefully rusticated first floor.

9.   In the quaint, narrow High Street is the timber-framed Recorder's House built in 1610 and close by is the house of Samuel Skey which was transformed in the 18th century from Tudor to Georgian.

10.   Tickenhill, the manor west of the town built by the Mortimers, was enlarged by Richard Duke of York who also provided Bewdley with its first bridge in 1447. His son Edward, Earl of March, the future Edward IV, lived for a time at Tickenhill, and granted the town a charter in 1472 in return for the support of Bewdley men at the Battle of Tewkesbury, where he finally destroyed the Lancastrian forces of Queen Margaret and brought to an end the Wars of the Roses.

In 1499, Prince Arthur, the eldest son of Henry VII, was betrothed by proxy to Catherine of Aragon at Tickenhill House. Shortly after his marriage the Prince died of pneumonia at Ludlow Castle and on the 25th April 1502 his body rested at Tickenhill on its way to Worcester Cathedral for burial there.

11.   Dowles Manor north of the town-a small Elizabethan house, sadly a fire casualty some years ago and at present undergoing restoration − possesses some of the best wall paintings of the period. They are largely stylised arabesques in grey and red with an Elizabethan lady and man.

12.   Ribbesford House south of the town was once the home of the powerful Beauchamp family, and later, of the 17th century poet

George Herbert. In World War II it was used for a time as the training centre for officers of the Free French Forces.

The little church of St. Leonard is interesting for its tympanum depicting a knight transfixing a monster with an arrow. The building was struck by lightning and had to be partially rebuilt in 1877 with columns of wood and stone. At the west end is a pleasant window by William Morris after a design by Burne-Jones.

13.   The caves in the sandstone rocks on the east side of the river below the town at Blackstone Rock were used as a hermitage in the Middle Ages, and also provided shelter for travellers who were held up when the river was too high to ford before the building of the 15th century bridge. Until the middle of the 19th century the Severn was tidal to this point, and vessels commonly moored here to await the tidal bore to carry them up to the quays at Bewdley.

INDEX

216